Contents

Bosham...a village by the sea
First published in Great Britain in 2006 by
HUGHENDEN PUBLICATIONS
Bosham, West Sussex

Text copyright© Angela Bromley-Martin
Illustrations copyright © Eric Hinkley

Photographs, except where otherwise acknowledged
from the collection of Angela Bromley-Martin

ISBN 0-9541395-1-8

The High Street 2005

Book design by Diana Greenwood Mead

Printed by
RPM PRINT & DESIGN
2-3 Spur Road, Quarry Lane, Chichester,
West Sussex PO19 8PR

Acknowledgements

For many years I have wanted to publish a book that would give not just the history of Bosham and its surroundings, but include details of the lives of the people who have lived here, how they have occupied themselves, the kind of houses in which they lived, the ghost stories and the legends that have been passed down from father to son; a book that would be easy to read as well as being as accurate as possible. The latter is proving the most difficult!

Historians have a difficult time for it depends largely on whose side they are when recounting their story, which books they have read for historical and other facts and the accuracy of those who recount the stories. Some years ago, on more than one occasion, I invited three elderly Bosham ladies to tea. One afternoon I showed them a 1903 photograph of the pupils at the village school - one in which they were all agreed they were pictured. But none of them could agree the names of the others in the picture, not even their own brothers, sisters, cousins or friends. The temperature in the room, as did their voices, rose higher and higher as they rebuked each other for apparently inaccurately identifying in the old photographs their then fellow classmates, even their own relations. I really wondered how I, a humble listener to these arguments, could possibly be sure that I would not make many errors in identifying people. When writing the captions for some of my collection of over 2,500 old photographs of the village, I will never be able to guarantee that I have named those pictured correctly. So while I have endeavored to be as accurate as possible, inevitably there will be some errors.

This book would not be as it is if it were not for the tremendous help I have had from so many people - those who have given me information about their families, their homes, their occupations and their recollections. Sheila Barton has also made a great contribution in her two chapters on Church visitors and Ghosts. There are too many to name individually - but to all of them I give my grateful thanks.

Then there are those who have laboriously read through the pages correcting any historical, grammatical or spelling errors: Kim Leslie of the West Sussex Record Office, Sir Jeremy Thomas, Christopher Bromley-Martin and Dilys Grey have all been of such tremendous help, by each reading through the chapters and putting me straight on many things - mistakes which I, like most writers, had been unaware of until they were pointed out.

Many of the sketches and drawings have been done painstakingly and carefully by Eric Hinkley. At one point he lost all his careful work when his computer crashed, but nothing daunted, he started again and I cannot thank him enough for his patience. John Pollock too has given me an enormous amount of help - answers to my questions often delivered to my door within a few minutes of the request. Finally to Diana Mead without whose help, encouragement, suggestions and hard work this book never would have been completed. To all of them I would like to say thank you.

Angela Bromley-Martin
January 2005

3

Bibliography

Book of Chichester ....Leslie Keating
Bosham ....David Beaumont
Bosham Church, Its Histories & Antiquities ....K.MacDermott
Bosham in the County of Sussex ...................C.J.Longcroft
Bosham: Ecclesia ....John Pollock
Boxgrove: History of a Sussex Village ....Boxgrove History Group
Brickmaking in Sussex ....M.Beswick
Bosham and its Berkeley Barons ....Maurice Hall
Chichester: a Documentary History ....Roy Morgan
Fishbourne: A Village History ....Rita Blakeney
Harold the King ....Helen Hollick
Harold Rex: ....John Pollock
Harold: the Last Anglo Saxon King ....Ian Walker
I Saw Two Englands ............................H.V.Morton
Looking Back in Sussex ....Arthur Stanley Cooke
Researching and Writing History ....David Dymond
St. Wilfrid of Ripon .............................J.S.Fletcher
Sussex ....Augustus Hare
Sussex the Garden by the Sea ....Arthur Mee
Sussex ....Ian Nairn & Nikolaus Pevsner
Victoria County History & many others.

The author would like to acknowledge and thank the following for the use of their photographs: Aerofilms, The West Sussex Record Office, The Berkeley Family Trust, The editor of The Chichester Observer, J.Colgate, Mark Jarrad, & John Pollock. Other photographs are by the author or from her photographic collection of pictures of Bosham

Note: CURRENCY CONVERSION

It is difficult to know how best to deal with the conversion from the old pounds, shillings and pence to decimal currency. It would be impossible to convert the old prices into today's equivalent value. Therefore throughout this book, in brackets, is placed, beside each old form of money, the straight calculation of the amount in decimal currency as follows:-

£sd	£p	£sd	£p
£1.0s0d	=£1.00	£0.1s.0d or 1/-	=5p
£0.15s0 or 15/-	=75p	£0.0s.6d	=$2^{1}/_{2}$p
£0.10s.0d or 10/-	=50p	£0.0.3d	=1p
£0.5s.0d or 5/-	=25p	£0.0.1d or 1d	=$^{1}/_{2}$p
£0.2s.6d or 2/6d	=$12^{1}/_{2}$p		

Preface

Oh Bells of Happy Bosham
For centuries long past,
Your welcome sound has cheered us on
When nearing home at last.
How often 'neath far foreign skies
We've longed to hear your call;
For the bells of Happy Bosham
Ring the sweetest chime of all.

Do you, my reader, ever stand at a favourite spot and wonder how different the view might have been one thousand, two thousand or even a million years ago?

My favourite view in the village of Bosham is at the top of School Rithe, one of the creeks of Chichester Harbour, only a few yards from the old National School of 1834. On the far right the spire of the Saxon church stands sentinel over a row of former fishermen's homes where, at times of high tides, the sea comes up to the windows of the little seaside cottages. To the left the road winds away around the corner; it too is covered by the sea at high tides. Between the two arms and beyond the sea grass, lie boats of every size and description; dinghies, fishing boats and luxury yachts – the scene an ever changing one as the tidal flow comes and goes, the sun shines brightly or not at all and the wind varies from flat calm to gale force. The setting has changed little in the last one thousand years, except for the church spire which has been there for only six hundred.

'Bosham is undoubtedly one of the most interesting spots in Sussex and in some respects, in England too' wrote Arthur Stanley Cooke in about 1912. It is dificult to write of a place so steeped in history, yet so small in area.In the early 1960s at Fishbourne, a village three miles east of Bosham the remains of a Roman palace was unearthed, the largest Roman edifice yet uncovered in north-west Europe.This find has resulted in Bosham itself becoming an even more popular place to visit.

All the year round visitors pour down to the heart of the village, many to drive around and be away in a few minutes, while others linger to sample the fare of The Anchor or settle down to a picnic perched on wobbly stools to savour the smells and ozone of sea and mud. Some set up easels and with paint and brush try to capture the ever-changing scene of sea and sky, mud and grass, boats and people. The earliest known paintings are those by Grimm in 1792 which are now preserved in the British Museum, while in the mid 19th century groups of painters came over from Paris to capture the local scene - artists are nothing new to Bosham!

Where did the name Bosham (pronounced Bozzam) come from? Through the centuries there are reputed to have been some twenty-eight different versions of the spelling of the name of the village/town - for in the 8th century Bosham was the sixth most important town in Sussex. There have been Boshenham, Bossenham, Buscham, Bossam and many others, although it was definitely recorded as Bosham in the Domesday Book of 1086. The name is probably derived from the Latin word 'boscus' meaning 'wood' and 'ham' meaning a hamlet. In short, a hamlet in the woods - Bosham has always been rich in oak woods, even to this day. (There has been a suggestion that Bosham was named after a local chieftain called Bosa, but he lived some years after Bosham had acquired its name.)

Having gone through the centuries as a fishing and farming community, it is now a thriving sailing centre to which every summer come dozens of enthusiasts, young and old, to launch their boats of every variety and enjoy the waters of Bosham, Chichester Harbour and beyond. There are the residents of every age, some of whose families have lived here for generations, some more recent arrivals who have jobs in one of the large cities and towns nearby. There are the weekenders who come to relax, a large proportion of whom eventually retire to their second home. Of such is the area made: an energetic society that is definitely in the 21st century but does not forget its history or its past. In 1969 the centre of the village was made into a Conservation Area.

So here within the pages of this book is written nearly everything that is known as well as interesting about this large village on the edge of Chichester Harbour. Not every single detail has been included, nor has the name of every individual who has played a part in the making of the village what it is today - a delightful place in which to live and love, relax and appreciate. I hope you will all enjoy reading it.

Angela Bromley-Martin

CHAPTER 2

The Early Centuries

Bosham's history goes back at least ten thousand years when Britain broke away from the continent of Europe to become an island, the southern portion of which was separated from Normandy by the English River and the Isle of Wight from mainland England by the Solent. The indentations that form what is now known as Chichester Harbour would have been a safe haven in which to settle, the oak woods providing the few inhabitants with timber for house and boat building, acorns for feeding the swine and the seas a plentiful supply of fish.

However, going back even further: a recent archaeological dig in a gravel pit at Boxgrove, a village eleven kilometres (seven miles) east of Bosham, found the bones of a man of half a million years ago which shows that this area has been inhabited for many thousands of years. The coastal plain south of the Downs, at that time, formed part of a vast savannah that stretched from here to Africa – bones of lions, elephants, rhinos, antelopes, as well as many other animals that now wander the grasslands of central Africa, have been found as a result of excavations in the area. Also found were many flint tools and hand axes used to butcher the meat; in fact it has been suggested that so many flints have been found there that it may have been the site of a local flint factory.

There is evidence that in about 4,000 B.C people arrived in this area with knowledge of agriculture. They used stone axes to cut down the oak forests where, with slashing and burning, they

The oak woods on Bosham Hoe, one of the few remaining areas of the Old Park Woods

were able to clear small areas in which to grow cereals. This development of the land progressed slowly through the Bronze and particularly the Iron Ages, for once iron tools were available it was easier to till the heavy clay soil of the area. There is evidence of trading in corn, cattle, silver and iron all along this coastal plain. With the prevailing wind south-westerly, either under oar or sail, given the right weather conditions, it would have been a relatively easy journey between what we now know as Normandy to the many safe anchorages

A Celtic head found in a pond in Bosham in the 1960s.

around the harbour, particularly in the deep waters of Bosham. Some years ago, a carved Celtic stone head was found in a pond in Bosham of such size that it could not have arrived in the roots of an imported tree! The Belgae and ancient Britons were also around here before the Romans arrived at the beginning of the 1st century.

The discovery of the Roman Palace at Fishbourne, only a few miles east of Bosham, gives greater credence to the belief that Bosham was an important centre in Roman times. At the time of writing there is a great controversy raging over whether the Claudian invasion of Britain in AD43 took place in Chichester Harbour instead of the long-held view that the landing was in Richborough, Kent. A number of Roman military buildings and artefacts have been unearthed around the Roman Palace, some of which pre-date AD43. The argument in favour of Richborough is the shorter distance between Boulogne and Richborough, where there is a great deal of evidence of Roman military activity. The journey from the Seine estuary to Chichester Harbour would however have taken much longer. The Atrebates, the tribe who occupied the area around Chichester under their Chief Verica (or Berikos), were known to be friendly to Rome, while the Cantiaci who lived in the Kent area of southern England, which included Richborough, were known to be hostile. To mount a military expedition of the size it is suggested, i.e. over 1,000 ships, 45,000 men plus military supplies, would have been a mammoth task. To get all these vessels into the small harbour of Richborough as well as feeding and supplying such a quantity of men in an hostile environment, would have been a formidable undertaking. It may well be that there was a two-pronged attack – one on the east coast at Richborough and the other into Chichester Harbour.

Whichever way future historians may decide where the Roman invasion took place, there is no doubt that the Romans did use and live in Bosham from the early 1st century. There was no natural water course to that area of the village which we know the Romans occupied. So it is likely that the brook, which is a man-made waterway, was built by the Romans and this aqueduct was to provide a water supply to the central part of the village for hundreds of years until mains water pipes were laid, beginning in the early 20th century. During renovations to the Mill House (picture Page 12), the building which is alongside the brook and not many yards from the church, a number of small Roman artefacts were found under the floor of the kitchen. In the 1960s in a little alleyway between the western boundary of the Mill House garden and Hope Cottage, the then Vicar of Bosham, the Rev. Bransby Jones, with Barry Goodinge, the publican of the Anchor Bleu, found a Roman road some fifty centimetres (18 inches) below the surface. In the church, the bases of the chancel arch are thought to be Roman, a survival from the Roman basilica which stood on the site. Basilicas were usually large rectangular buildings, often with a circular apse at one end, built by the Romans for use as an assembly hall or a court of law. It must have been a substantial building as a very large Roman head was dug up in the churchyard in the early 19th century. There are many theories as to whose statue it could be. It might be that of one of the Roman Emperors - Claudius,

Vespasian or Trajan - or is of a later date and could be that of the Saxon god Woden. Its size and worn condition suggests that it could have graced the top of a pillar outside the entrance to the Roman basilica, on the foundations of which stands the parish church of today.

In the mid-19th century a Roman villa and amphitheatre were found in the area of Broadbridge Farm while more recently coins from the 3rd century have been found in the vicinity. Roman artefacts were also found in the garden of the White Swan Inn. Another stone

The Roman head which was found in the churchyard in the 19th century & which is now in the District Museum in Chichester.

head was found a few years ago in the garden of Broadbridge Mill. However, it was in too good a condition to be Roman but rather is an 18th century copy, made in Italy and brought back to England by some wealthy gentleman after doing the grand tour of the continent.

A number of Roman brickworks have been found around the harbour and there is a possibility that one of these could have been at Furzefield on Bosham Hoe. The ruins of a brickyard which was in use prior to 1638 when the shape of the bricks was changed, are still to be seen. The clay soil (brickearth) together with adequate sources of wood and furze for firing the kilns with its close proximity to the water were all features the Romans sought for successful brick making. The Romans almost certainly used Furzefield Creek as an anchorage for their vessels, protected as it is from the prevailing south-west wind – pieces of Roman mortar have been found in the area.

There are along the south shore of the creek amongst the saltings, various indentations in the form of boat-like shapes which may be the hulls of Roman vessels. More details of this conjecture can be found on Page 220. W.E.P. Done in his book 'Looking Back in Sussex' writes that the Romans almost certainly had a highly efficient communication system whereby the movements of ships sailing along the south coast could be passed to either Portchester to the west or Anderida

(Pevensey) in the east. A lookout on a lighthouse or similar erection on the Owers Bank (now under water) would have signalled this information to Bracklesham from where there is evidence of a Roman road that ran straight through to Birdham. Where today's road between these two places diverts from the straight line, there are the remains of a Roman carriageway in the fields, which adds credence to his theory. From here, the information would have been signalled across to Longmore Point on Bosham Hoe, then via Hoe Lane northwards to the top of Downs and then to whichever direction the information was required. The ruins of Roman signal towers have been found on the Downs.

While the Romans would have enjoyed such luxuries as mosaic floors, central heating and running water in their houses, built of locally made bricks and roofs of clay tiles, the local Britons would have had wooden-framed wattle and daub houses with thatched roofs. One can imagine these rectangular houses lining the edge of the harbour

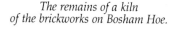

The remains of a kiln
of the brickworks on Bosham Hoe.

above the high water mark, with small wooden fishing boats hauled up the slipways alongside the huts. For the farmers, they would have used iron-tipped wooden ploughs to till their fields and have stored the grain in similar buildings to those in which they lived. Aside from fish and grain, there would have been meat available in the form of wild boar and deer, the skins of which would have provided them with clothing and footwear. Salt, essential for the preservation of their winter food, came from salt pans known to have existed at the top of the Cut Mill Creek and possibly in School Rithe by the old school. They would have had horses and carts for moving their goods from place to place. To the Romans, this coastal area of southern England was a highly desirable place to live, as can be judged by the number of villas that have been located around here – as many as five in the Bosham area. Politically the region was peaceful with an agreeable climate and there was everything available in material terms: cheap labour, good soil for growing crops and animal fodder, excellent wood supplies as well as easy access to the continent to obtain luxury items. The Romans built what today we would call stately homes where they could produce their own metal work (there is evidence of a small iron industry) the local clay was excellent for making pottery while there was a plentiful supply of fish. There is also known to have been a substantial oyster industry. It is also interesting to note that almost all the present footpaths eastwards from the church all lead towards the Roman Palace. Perhaps the deep water anchorage of Bosham was easier for docking ships than the often shallow waters of Fishbourne although the former was a longer distance from Chichester. Officially, the Romans ceased governing these islands in the 5th century, but many settled here, perhaps having married local girls and did not wish return to the heat of southern Europe.

A model of what the basilica, thought to have been built by the Romans, would have looked like in the 3rd century.

The Mill House reflected in the waters of the brook which runs alongside the church wall, which is on the right.

CHAPTER 3

After the Romans

With the departure of the Romans, the coastal area, indeed the whole of England, went into decline. There had been endless attacks along the coast, which the Romans no longer had the resources to counter for they were being threatened on their far eastern frontiers. Within two hundred years of the Romans leaving these shores their language, law and economy had disappeared. Jutes, Saxons, Angles and Vikings attacked the towns along the coastal plain relentlessly, terrifying the local inhabitants and forcing them to abandon the towns to form straggling villages in the foothills of the Downs and along the coast. The roads that had been built by the Romans fell into disrepair, slowly the forests became impenetrable and contact with inhabitants north of the Downs ceased. For the next fourteen hundred years trade and communications were principally by sea, usually to the continent. From Bosham it was easier and quicker to reach the Seine than the Thames or London.

In AD477, Aella landed in Chichester Harbour with his three sons, Cymen, Wlencing and Cissa, the latter after whom Chichester is named – Cissa's city. Aella formed the Kingdom of the South Saxons. The methods of farming as used by the Saxons in the 5th and 6th centuries were to remain largely unchanged for the next one thousand years, while the principal crops grown during those years were mainly wheat, barley and oats.

By the 8th century, Bosham was the sixth most important town in Sussex, in spite of the continuing raids by the Vikings. The Vikings are thought to have attacked Chichester in 894, while the Danes attacked a year later, resulting in two hundred people being killed and the countryside ravaged; this no doubt included Bosham. So angry was King Alfred (reigned 871–99) over these continuous raids on the coastal villages that he ordered that burhs, or forts, should be built all along the coast, one of these fortifications being at Chichester.

One can see the narrow entrance to Chichester Harbour from Bosham church tower today. During the centuries that the harbour was attacked the villagers almost certainly had a lookout of some sort somewhere in the vicinity of the present church possibly on the foundations of either the Roman basilica or the present church tower. This would have given the villagers a few hours warning of any possible raid. On one of these raids an incident took place which gave rise to the legend of the Bosham bell, details of which can be found in Chapter 15

Alfred died in 899. Unfortunately his qualities were not sustained by his immediate successors. But 117 years on, in 1016, the Danish King Canute, or Knut, at the early age of 22, became the first king to unite all of England. He proved to be efficient and fair minded, so England prospered under his rule with twenty years of peace. Canute's sister, Estrid, married Duke Robert of Normandy, the father of the illegitimate William the Bastard, afterwards known as the Conqueror. Canute established his capital in Winchester, only a day's ride from Bosham, where he was thought to have had a manor house. In 1017, he married Emma, the widow of King Aethelred, the Unready, who bore him a son.

Bosham is one of a number of places where Canute (reigned 1016-35) is alleged to have sat on a chair, surrounded by his courtiers and ordered the tide to retreat which it failed to do. The concept behind this was that even he, the great King of England and Denmark, had no power over the waters of the sea.

Bosham, along with areas in East Anglia and around Plymouth in Devon as well the area south of the South Downs, has an above average number of sun hours as well as good soil, resulting in high yielding corn of excellent quality. As far back as Roman times, corn from the coastal plain of Wessex fed some of the Roman armies of north-west Europe. As a result farmers were always looking for places where they could reclaim land within this high sunshine area to increase corn yield.

Cut Mill Creek, which runs north from the Quay at Bosham, dries out at low tide. so it would have been a good area to reclaim. A likely explanation for the Canute legend is that a dyke was built across the harbour just above the Quay and this area was reclaimed for farming. The Saxon word for dyke is char, because at that time the stakes that were used to build dykes were charred; this was the only known way of

Mud Wall

preserving the posts that were hammered into the salt water ground, behind which mud and straw were thrown to form the walls of the dykes. One can only think that Canute's dyke was not a very successful one and before long it was breached as a result of a hurricane or exceptionally high tides, the weakness being that the dyke faced the prevailing south westerly winds. There is another possibility that the use of the word 'chair' in the legend may have evolved from the Saxon name given to earthen banks which were built, centuries ago, to keep the sea out of the fields and which were known as 'chairs'. (The effect of throwing the earth on to a bank could have left a chair-shaped bank.)

Some seven hundred years after Canute, a dyke 4.50 metres (15 feet) high and 507 metres (550 yards) long was built and Cut Mill Creek reclaimed for farming. An elderly lady recalled in the 1970s her mother telling her that in her childhood (in the 1860s) she remembered seeing the ruins of a farmhouse in the middle of Cut Mill Creek. In the 18th and early 19th centuries there is documentation that the Lord of the Manor gave agricultural rights for farming this reclaimed land. For a few years there was a roadway along the top of the dyke wall which enabled Chidham children to attend Sunday School in Bosham. In 1825 a very high tide backed by strong south westerly winds, breached this dyke and water flooded back into the creek – the Lord of the Manor then gave fishermen the rights to use the area for oyster fishing. The remains of that dyke which

An aerial photo of October 1949, showing the remains of the 18th century dyke (now known as Mud Wall). The land reclaimed north of this dyke was farmed for some thirty years. (photo by Aerofilms)

ran from Chidham across to the area of the old shipyard, a few yards from the church, is today known as Mud Wall. There have been other places in Chichester Harbour where attempts have been made to reclaim land; only one has survived the centuries and that one faces north.

One of the few people who rose to prominence during Canute's reign was Earl Godwin, father of Harold and who was later to become the father-in-law of Edward the Confessor. Canute created Godwin Earl of Wessex, the area of England south of the Thames and which was considered the most important earldom in England, a title normally held by the monarch. After Godwin's death, Harold became the 2nd Earl Godwin and, after the death of Edward, King Harold II of 1066 fame. After Canute's death in 1035, first his son Harold I, The Harefoot , became king followed by Harold's half brother, Hardicanute. Luckily neither reigned for long as both were disasters. It was Hardicanute's half brother, Edward the Confessor, who then inherited the throne of England.

On Canute's death the Manor of Bosham was given to the See of Canterbury. The Manor was a very rich one, much coveted by Godwin, so the story goes that he, Godwin, acquired this manor by a trick. It was usual for men to ask a blessing from the Archbishop of Canterbury, using the words 'da mihi basium' (Give me your blessing). Godwin went to Archibishop Agilnotus, so it is alleged, and pretended to ask for the usual blessing. Instead he said 'Da mihi Boseam' 'Give me

A section from the Bayeux Tapestry, embroidered in the 11th century, it is thought, to the order of Queen Matilda, wife of William the Conqueror. It shows Harold , in 1064 , having a blessing in Bosham Church and a feast in the Manor House

Bosham'. Whatever it was he said he appears to have acquired the Lordship of the Manor. When, many years later, he was accused of dishonesty in acquiring this Manor, he denied it saying that if he had lied God would smite him. He promptly collapsed and died five days later from a stroke. Godwin had three sons: Sweyn, Earl of Hereford, his eldest son, was the black sheep of the family. He carried off the Abbess of Leominster, whom he married and who bore him a number of children. He was banished from England but returned some years later to Bosham when he took, as a hostage, his cousin, Beorn, whom he later murdered in Dartmouth. He was killed at Stamford Bridge. Harold, his second son, who was to become Harold II, was born and lived in Bosham with his common law wife, Edith Swan-neck, by whom he had a number of children. There is controversy as to where Harold had his manor house – there are the remains of Saxon walls with windows and doorways to the north of the church in the grounds of the present Manor House. There is another suggestion that Harold's manor was south of the church in the area that was later occupied by the Austin Canons.

There is in Bayeux in Normandy, an appliquéd embroidery commissioned by William the Conqueror's half brother, Bishop Odo, and probably worked by nuns in Canterbury. In the Bayeux Tapestry, Harold is shown, in 1064, having a feast in the Manor House, a blessing service in the church before setting out for Normandy. The object of the journey was to parley with William the Bastard as to who should have the throne of England on the death of

before setting out for Normandy to parley with William as to who should have the throne of England on the death of Edward the Confessor. (Courtesy of City of Bayeux)

TOWER FACES

N2

NW

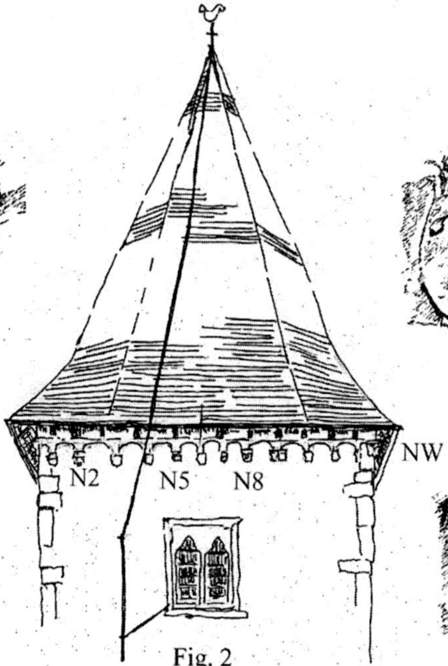

N5

NW

N2   N5   N8

NW

N8

Fig. 2

17 Decorative elements →

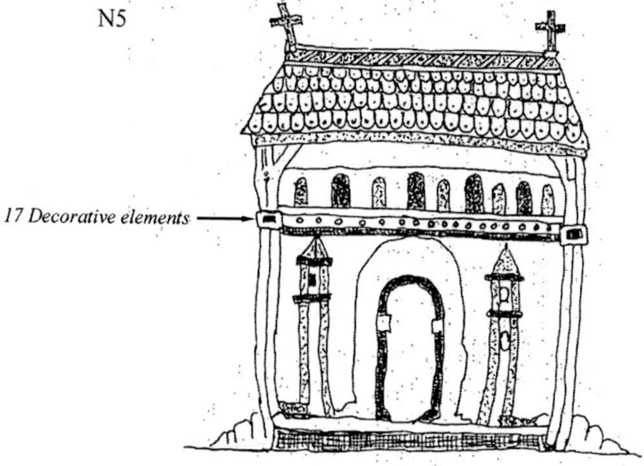

Fig. 1

In his booklet, 'Bosham Ecclesia', John Pollock seeks to show the accuracy of the Bayeux Tapestry. One of the examples he gives is that of the similarity of the view of seventeen decorative elements (heads) depicted in the tapestry in 1066 (fig.1) and that of the apparent same heads as seen today (Fig.2). Four of the heads, under the eaves of the north wall of the church tower, are illustrated

Edward the Confessor, for Edward and Edith were childless. Harold kept his fleet in Bosham, where some of his ships were almost certainly built. Harold was shipwrecked on the Normandy coast, taken into custody by William's half brother, Bishop Odo. It was some time before Harold was released into William's care and custody. The story goes that before William would allow Harold to return to England, Harold was forced to sign an oath that he, Harold, would not take the throne of England on Edward's death. Harold was also forced into marriage with William's niece, who bore him a son born after his death, although the historians maintain that his true love was always Edith the Swan-neck whom, it is thought, he never married. In 1066 Harold II, who had had himself crowned King in Westminster Abbey earlier in the year, was killed at the Battle of Hastings and William the Conqueror took over the Royal Manor of Bosham. Some of Harold's house carls (free peasants) were Men of Bosham, many of whom died with him at Hastings. It would have been considered dishonourable for a Saxon warrior to live after his Lord had been killed in battle. Domesday Book, compiled twenty years after Hastings, shows a marked decline in Bosham's population compared with the numbers in Godwin's time.

A sketch from the Illustrated London News of 1888 showing the windmill on Cut Mill Creek - an area that is now called Windmill Fields. In 1970 an elderly resident of Bosham recalled that as a child she had played in the ruins of the old windmill.

Interior of Holy Trinity church, showing the chancel arch (similar to one depicted in the Bayeux tapestry). At the eastern end is the Early English window, said to be one of the finest examples in this country.

CHAPTER 4

The Followers of the Faith

As one sits in one of the Victorian wooden pews in the parish church of The Holy Trinity, slowly the history of the building unfolds before one's eyes – the Roman bases to the Saxon chancel arch, the Norman stonework, the magnificent Early English east window, the pulpit made from recycled wood from the church roof and finally the Elizabeth ll wrought iron banisters around the chapel of All Hallowes.

Here nearly two thousand years ago stood a Roman basilica, a rectangular building with, at its eastern end some experts believe, a blank east wall, while others think that there may have been a circular apse in the Roman tradition – a section of a partly filled-in window can be seen on the north wall close by the chancel arch which could have been part of that apse.

Bede in his Ecclesiastical History of the English Nation, tells how St. Wilfrid came to Bosham in 681 and found a Celtic monk named Dicul, together with six disciples, endeavouring to convert the locals to Christianity without much apparent success. There are many ideas of where Dicul had his monastery, for Bede speaks of a small monastery at a place called 'Bosanham' surrounded by woods and the sea. It is thought that the site of Dicul's little monastery may have been a mile or so inland of the church behind Crede Farm where early maps have an entry marked 'site of monastery'.

A model showing what the church might have looked like after it was converted from a Roman basilica to a place of Christian worship in about 850 A.D.

Even if Dicul did not have much success in converting the heathen of Bosham, others did, for by the 7th century most of the English kingdoms had been converted to Christianity. The present church dates back to about 850 at the time when Christianity had been established in this country. No doubt this led to King Alfred, King of Wessex (848–99), issuing general instructions that all former Roman basilicas should be repaired and converted into Christian churches. This change was evidently made in Bosham. A recent survey of the fabric of the church suggests that there is a considerable amount of Quarr stone, Bembridge limestone and Mixon rock from off Selsey Bill, as well as Caen stone. The original north and south walls of the earlier building were where the present pillars stand and were added in the 11th century. The chapel of All Hallowes built over the crypt was dedicated in October 1959. The chancel was built in three stages. The first shows the rather untidy Saxon stonework and it was during this period, 1040-50, that the chancel arch was inserted into the east wall. The Bayeux Tapestry, the historical embroidery, shows the chancel arch as we see it today. The next one-third of the chancel is of the Norman herringbone style while the third section is Early English which includes the beautiful east window added between 1220 and 1280, said to be one of the finest examples of its kind in this country. The inner doors of the south entrance are the original ones dating back to the 14th century, when the porch was added. The outer doors were replaced in 1906.

The tower too was built in four stages, the first two being of the same date as the original church, i.e. 9th century, and probably formed part of an archway of a porticus or porch of a main entrance on the west side of the church. The third stage, used as a bell chamber, was added in the 10th or early 11th century, while the fourth stage was built between 1056-66. The shingled spire was added in the 15th century. Canute (reigned 1016-35) had been brought up in the Christian faith and was a known benefactor of churches. It was during his time that the church in Bosham was enlarged.

During the Saxon period, a triangular headed door at the western end of the church opened out from the second floor of the east wall of the tower on to a gallery in the nave. This balcony may have been used for seating important people during church services. If this royal box was used by such a distinguished person as Godwin, Earl of Wessex, Lord of the Manor, then it must have been here before 1053, the year that Godwin died. Later this gallery was used by musicians accompanying the congregation during hymn singing before there was an organ, after which the balcony was removed. Alongside this doorway is a small window, a squint, from where the verger would have been able to see the altar and thus the right moment during Mass for him to ring the Sanctus bell.

In 1865 when the floor of the nave was being re-laid, a Saxon stone coffin was found at the foot of the chancel steps. In it were the bones of an eight-year old girl. Stories had long been told that a daughter of Canute's had been drowned in the brook and buried in the church. If it was not Canute's daughter, who else could it be? She must have been a very important person to be buried in such a prime place and in such a superior coffin. In the Easter Sepulchre alongside the organ there is the stone effigy of a little girl dressed in royal robes of the 13th century, two hundred years after Canute. One of her feet rests on a lion of England, the other on a raven, the national emblem of Denmark, for Canute was King of Denmark as well as England. This effigy fits the top of the coffin exactly and

clearly was made for it. The Plantagenet King Edward 1st (reigned 1272–1307) was known to have visited Bosham many times. He was also known to order stone effigies of anyone he felt was not being venerated enough. Did Edward commission this statue to the little girl, thrown into the churchyard on Henry VIII's Dissolution of the Monasteries and later replaced in the church, albeit not on the coffin?

In 1954, when, once again, work was being done to the floor of the nave, a second Saxon stone coffin was found alongside that

The scene taken in 1954 when both the coffins sited at the foot of the chancel steps had been opened in the presence of the vicar, the Rev. Bransby-Jones. Dean Hussey of Chichester Cathedral, and Dr. Langhorne, the local doctor.

(Photo courtesy of the Chichester Observer)

of the little princess. It was a long held view that this second coffin, which again must have been of an important person in such a prodigious stone coffin at the foot of the chancel steps, was that of Earl

23

Godwin. The chronicles say that the first earl was buried in the Minster at Winchester, though his body has never been found. In this second coffin were the thigh and pelvic bones of a powerfully built man, about five feet in height and sixty years old, which answered the description of the 2nd Earl Godwin. (It is often difficult from ancient bones to give a precise age of a man over twenty.) Harold would have been in his late forties (his birth date is not known but is thought to be around 1020.) John Pollock who has done a great deal of research on Harold and has written a small booklet *Harold: Rex*, is of the opinion that these are the remains of Harold, who on the death of his father had become the 2nd Earl Godwin. It was always understood that Harold was buried in Waltham Abbey, the church he founded in Essex.

Both Gyda, Harold's mother, and his common law wife, Edith Swan-neck, lived in Bosham. William the Conqueror, after Harold's death at Hastings in 1066, was anxious that Harold should not be made a martyr – did William allow Edith to take the body and bury it secretly in Bosham church – the absence of a skull and a left leg coincides with the details as shown in the tapestry of Harold's death at the Battle of Hastings? William de Poitiers wrote later that Harold was buried by the sea. So could it be that indeed Earl Godwin is buried here – but it is the 2nd Earl Godwin, Harold II of England.

In 1042, Edward the Confessor became King of England (reigned 1042–66) and during his lifetime gave the ecclesiastical part of the Manor of Bosham, which included the patronage of the church as well as the western portion of the manor, to his chaplain, Osbern FitzOsbern. In 1072, FitzOsbern became Bishop of Exeter, while Godwin retained the eastern half of the manor which, in due course, passed to Harold and then to the Conqueror. On the death of Bishop Osbern in 1103, the patronage reverted to the crown and Bosham became a royal peculiar under the jurisdiction of King Henry 1st, youngest son of the Conqueror. But not for long, for Henry (reigned 1100-35) granted the church with its portion of the manor, to Bishop Warlewaste of Exeter. This Bishop formed a college of a dean and five secular canons in Bosham. These were monks who ministered to the lay community in which they lived as well as to other churches in the area. It was neither a teaching order nor a closed order. These included the prebends (a portion of the revenue of the cathedral or church granted to the canons of a church as a stipend) of Bosham Parochial, Appledram, Chidham, Funtington, Walton and Westbrooke. In fact until 1408 and 1417 respectively, the dead of Appledram and Funtington had to be brought to Bosham for burial which could be difficult, particularly in bad weather. Arrangements were made for these villages to bury their own dead but only on payment to the Vicar of Bosham of one penny for each adult and a halfpenny for each child buried other than in Bosham. These payments seem to have been forgotten over the years for no recent incumbent of Bosham has ever heard of their existence.

In about 1220, the then Pope, Honorius III, decreed that, in order to finance the crusaders, all churches in the kingdom must have a chest into which all those who were unable to go on a crusade to the Holy Land, should put contributions of either money or goods to pay for those who could. The chest in the chancel is one such and dates from 1220. For returning crusaders, Bosham was often the first church they came to on landing on English soil, where they could pray and thank God for their safe return. The evidence of returning pilgrims blunting their swords can be seen in the scratch marks on the south entrance of the church. The graffiti seen on some of the pillars, particularly near the font, are no modern day vandalism but the scratchings depicting various Christian symbols drawn by these crusaders. The Fishbourne Chantry Chapel was founded in 1330.

The canons used the chancel of the church as their chapel, a rood screen or curtain was erected in front of the chancel arch and a new altar installed at the foot of the chancel steps. There is a pew end beside the organ in the chancel which is the only surviving relic of the

monks. The monks had their cells where now stand the former poor houses, afterwards renamed Harbour Cottages. There is more than one account that these cells were connected to an underground passage that ran from there to the church – as a result of incursions from the sea, the church end of that passageway is now under four feet of concrete. The vaults of Quay Cottage, opposite the mill on the Quay, now the Bosham Sailing Club, are also thought to have been part of the college. All that remains of the college buildings, which were situated on the south side of the church, is the little doorway immediately opposite the main south

The old doorway leading into the area where the monks cells were situated and which is thought to be the only remaining evidence of the little monastery

entrance of the church, now part of the garden of Brook House. These buildings were returned to the ownership of the church after the dissolution of the monasteries. One of these buildings became the Parsonage House and was used as the vicarage until 1840 when it was condemned and a new one built at the top of Walton Lane, now called Walton House. On the site of the old Parsonage House, two cottages known as 1 and 2 Church Cottages, were built in its place. The monks had a guard house attached to the church, now the sacristy, where a permanent watch was kept against robbers who might steal the church valuables. The sacristy consists of two floors where the duty monk could live in a self contained maisonette on the ground floor of which there is still a cooking range. It is interesting to think that security in the church was a problem eight hundred years ago!

Once again Bosham, which was a Royal Free Chapel, came under the jurisdiction of the Bishop of Exeter and outside the control of the Bishop of Chichester. This was a tremendous thorn in the side of the Bishop of Chichester, who, not surprisingly, resented having a church only a few miles from his cathedral and technically in his diocese but not under his control. In 1120, a later Bishop of Exeter, Bishop Stapledon, signified his intention of visiting his church and college in Bosham to which Bishop Langton of Chichester objected very strongly. But to no avail and something stronger than words were exchanged by the followers of the two opposing bishops at South Harting, a village about ten miles north-west of Chichester, on the border of the diocese. Bishop Langton threatened Stapledon with excommunication but the latter, undaunted, continued on his way to Bosham.

Bishop Langton carried out his threat. The Dean and Chapter of Chichester assembled in the Cathedral together with other church dignitaries and Bishop Stapledon was formally excommunicated. However, common sense soon prevailed and an agreement was made whereby the Bishop of Exeter retained the patronage while the Bishop of Chichester had the right of visitation and authority over the church at Bosham in the same way that he had over any other church or priest in his diocese.

The Pipe Roll of 1156 gives Bosham as the only manor strictly a Crown manor and owned by the king. It is important to distinguish between the royal manor of Bosham from the valuable chapelry of Bosham, as it was then termed, with its own estates owned at that time by the Bishop of Lisieux. The reason why for some thirteen years Bosham came under the jurisdiction of this Bishop was that during the dispute between Thomas à Becket, Archibishop of Canterbury, and Henry 2nd in 1163, the Bishop of Exeter sided with Becket, so Henry, in fury, in 1164 put Bosham under the jurisdiction of the Bishop of Lisieux in Normandy, where it remained until 1177.

To return to the monks, who were reported to be a somewhat

1. *Modern view of the other side of the doorway shown on page 25*

2 3 & 4. *Three of Grimms' paintings from 1782 of Bosham church and of what became known as the Parsonage House.*

2. *The section that was occupied until 1840 by the vicar.*

3. *The other half of the building, which was demolished at an earlier time.*

4. *The church with the Parsonage House on the left (note the masts of a vessel behind) and to the right, the Mill House.*

irreligious bunch of men. They were accused of not holding their Masses regularly or on time – in fact one was dismissed for visiting gambling houses and for living in sin with a Bosham widow! They failed to maintain the fabric of the church with the result that sometime in the 15th century, the roof fell in. Unable to pay for the roof to be restored as it was, a flat roof was made. Some of the corbels which held the wooden beams for that roof are still to be seen in the chancel of the church today. They probably represent the figured heads of those who worked in the church, like carpenters and stonemasons. One of them is of a priest

The interior of the church showing the flat roof. This was restored to its original height in 1865 when major renovations were made.

sticking out his tongue! In 1865 the roof was restored to its original position as it is today. So it would appear that in Bosham's case, Henry VIII had good reason

for dissolving this little monastery in 1536.

Bosham was a very wealthy church so was a very good source of income for the greedy Henry VIII and afterwards for his son, Edward VI. Everything of any value, such as silver vessels, books and vestments, was confiscated and sold, the monies raised going to the crown.

On the right on the inside of the entrance to the church there is Herbert of Boseham's tomb. Born in Bosham, Herbert was Thomas à Becket's secretary but on the orders of his superior left Canterbury a few days before Becket's murder in Canterbury Cathedral in 1170. Herbert wrote the life of St. Thomas of Canterbury, running to some seven volumes. Herbert later became Archibishop of Benevento and almost certainly died in Italy. It is most unlikely that Herbert is buried here; moreover the stone covering the tomb is one from an altar dated some two hundred years after Herbert's death. In one of his

An etching by Rouse. The original line of the roof (restored in 1865) can be seen to the east side of the tower.

poems, Tennyson wrote:-

'Better have been
A fisherman at Bosham, my good Herbert,
Thy birthplace – the sea – creek –
the petty rill
That falls into it – the green field –
the gray church –
The simple lobster-basket, and the mesh'

A corbel on the south wall of the chancel depicting the face of a monk sticking out his tongue

The Norman font is 13th century, made of Purbeck and Sussex marble. In 1236, the Archibishop of Canterbury ordered that all fonts should have locked lids. This was to prevent people taking the holy water and using it for improper purposes. The staples of the lock are still there.

During the mediaeval period, churches became the centre of the local community, a village hall in effect. Local foods were sold and beer brewed in the church while on feast days dancing and games took place in the churchyard. Any money raised from the sale of beer or anything else during these happy times went towards the upkeep of the church.

After the dissolution of the monasteries, the buildings were granted to Vincent Calmady, a layman and then to Sir Richard Sackville who in 1536 ceded them to the Dean and Chapter of Chichester Cathedral in exchange for the dissolved Priory of Wilmington in East Sussex. The patronage of the living of Bosham remained with the Dean and Chapter until 1840, when by Act of Parliament the patronage was transferred to the Bishop of Chichester where it remains to this day.

From the time of the dissolution of the college, the church was organised in much the same way as most of the parish churches in England. Bosham had a vicar, sometimes a curate, as well as a sexton, parish clerk and churchwardens who were all very

The Reverend Henry Mitchell.

important people within the community. One of the more famous incumbents was Henry Mitchell who was vicar for over fifty years (1845 – 1902) and before that for a few years, curate to the previous vicar, George How. Henry Mitchell was the first incumbent to live in the then new vicarage, now Walton House, with his wife and six children.

From being the very wealthy church it had been before the dissolution, Bosham became very poor and all sorts of means had to be found to maintain the fabric of the building. At one time the Dean and Chapter agreed to give Bosham church £370 per annum for repairs. Then in 1633 a new agreement was made whereby all the income from the Bosham estates would go to the church for its maintenance. In January 1638 the church steeple was struck by lightning and caught fire. With no money, it was suggested that the steeple be pulled down. The money was found to repair it, however. It appears that it is necessary to repair the tower and steeple every fifty years – an expensive item in the church finances.

When Richard Barwell died – he had earlier bought the estate from John Frankland – his executors sold the rights of the estate to Charles Cheesman, yeoman. By doing so, the Cheesman family became the lay rectors of the Chancel as well as the Coroner and Chamberlain for the village; in 1937 the position of lay rector was taken over by the Ecclesiastical Commissioners, with whom it still remains. The Cheesman family resided in Rectory Farm, now called Strange Hall, while the tithes were collected in the nearby barn. The Cheeseman family have a vault under the chancel of the parish church where many members of the family are buried.

There are many fields and properties in Bosham which retain names linked to the church because the income so derived was paid to the church – Church Field, Church Farm, Creed Farm, Critchfield, Chantry Field and many others.

In about 1810 the whole church was plastered and painted in terracotta. This was removed during the 1865 refurbishment, though a small section remains in the window in the north-west corner of the nave. The church seems to have avoided the excesses of the Victorian period and remained very plain, probably due to lack of funds to produce anything very ornate. Major repair work was done to the church in 1903-4 when the good wood left over from the repairs to roof and tower was used to make the present pulpit. One of the church bells was also repaired; before the bell was replaced in the bell tower, the infant son of one of the churchwardens, George Brown, the mill

In recent years there have been a number of surveys and studies made of the Parish Church and its history. Many have sought to disprove the accuracy of previous surveys and the opinion of other historians.

Amongst the accounts these experts have sought to question are the authenticity of whether the church was built on the remains of a Roman basilica, whether the two coffins were of King Canute's daughter and possibly that of King Harold, even questioning whether King Canute himself ever visited or lived in the town. Maybe one day in the future these stories will be proven one way or the other.

As Professor Frank Barlow of Exeter University once wrote 'Very few things in history can be proved'. There are, however, probabilities…

30

owner, was christened in the upturned bell by the vicar, Kenneth MacDermott. The names of the vicar and the then two churchwardens, the other being John Heaver, whose descendants still own property in the area, were inscribed on the outside of the bell. In the same year John Kearvell, the verger and carpenter, repaired the church tower for £128.5.8d. (£128.33p), which had to be paid in instalments which gives an idea of the state of the church finances at the time. More work was done to the church in 1907 when a new organ and heating were installed.

A pew end dating back to the time of the monks.

The vicar, Kenneth MacDermott, instituted a number of new ideas after he arrived in 1902. He started a monthly parish magazine, now called Bosham Life, which has continued ever since, listing all the village activities planned for the following month. Until recently the editor has been the Vicar of the Parish Church and now lists the activities of the other two churches, the Congregational church, which, during

The Rev. Kenneth MacDermott, vicar of Bosham 1902 to 1915, and the cover of the first Parish Magazine, which he started in 1902

the last century, became the United Reformed Church, and also of the Roman Catholic church

In order to raise money for all these improvements the new vicar started the church fetes, which raised hundreds of pounds and which continue to this day as a major annual event in the village. He also initiated services at Broadbridge by having evensong in the vicarage for those people who lived in the northern end of the village around Broadbridge. This led to St. Nicholas Hall being built in Brook Avenue on land at one time owned by the previous vicar, Mr. Mitchell, at a cost of £3,870 some of the money of which came from a large legacy left by the Reverend Rochfort Wade on his death. He had been Vicar of Bosham between 1915-22. This vicar had also set up a charity for £200 in memory of his wife, who had predeceased him, to be distributed between the four oldest men and four oldest women in the parish. St Nicholas Hall was dedicated in 1951 and evensong is held there every Sunday

The western view of the church interior showing the 'squint' a small window, left above the west door. From here the verger could see the priest at the altar and the right moment to ring the sanctus bell.

evening, while during the week many organisations make use of the hall as a meeting place. Mr. MacDermott left Bosham in 1915 to become Vicar of Selsey and a Canon of Chichester Cathedral. Mr. MacDermott wrote a number of books, one being *Bosham Church: Its History and Antiquities.*

Today Bosham Parish Church goes on much as it has done over the last four hundred years. Bosham was one of the first parish churches to have a female priest – Jan Emerson arrived in 1994 and for eight years was the Assistant Curate. 2002 also saw the installation of new lighting as well as a new central heating system. Finances are still a problem but parishioners are making regular contributions for the upkeep of the church by gift aid, which enables the church to reclaim tax, thereby increasing the donations. The church still remains the centre of the village, with well-supported services and thousands of people coming from all parts of the world to walk around this two thousand year old edifice; their donations also contributing to the finances for the upkeep of the church. (See chapter 5.)

There are two other denominations which each have a church in the village, for not everyone went to the parish church. The United Reformed Church, more recently known as the Fishermens' Chapel, a name given to it by the original worshippers in 1837, have their chapel at the corner of Bosham Lane opposite Church Farm House.

In 1834 a large group from the village built the Congregational Church in Bosham Lane. Looking back into the history of this church, it seems that in the early 1800s, there was a growing band of parishioners in the village, as well as all over the country, who were becoming disenchanted with the Established Church. In the Church Book of 1825, there is written 'The village of Bosham was, until the year 1812, proverbial for ignorance and wickedness, there being no Gospel either in the Established Church or out of it'. So, in that year a group of locals, under the leadership of Dr. David Bogue, a founder member of the Hampshire Congregational Union, organised weekly services in the oyster barn on Shore Road known at the time as the Storehouse, across the pathway from the Anchor and where now stands a house called 'Oysters'. The numbers joining this break-away group increased until it was felt that they needed a chapel of their own.

In 1837 a piece of land was purchased for £115 which included a

The programme for the Thanksgiving Festival service following the renovations to the church.

cottage, Chapel Cottage, and building commenced. The total cost of the building was £500; a debt that was not to be paid off until 1872. In 1875 a schoolroom was built while in 1928 a manse was purchased in Brook Avenue for the incumbent. By 1937, under the Minister, the Rev. H.W. Gurney, the Congregational Church had a flourishing Sunday School. Alfred White, ever since he could remember until he died in 1983, was a regular

child received a book of some kind. For many years, the Congregationalists also had their annual church fetes in the Manor House grounds

One of the memorial tablets in the church is to Mr. William Norris, who served the church as Sunday School teacher for over sixty years and lived in Chapel Cottage. One hundred years later, in 1972, with the Union of the Congregational and Presbyterian Churches, the church became the

Mr. Norris, one of the village carriers. He lived in Chapel Cottage,(on the left), and was the Sunday School teacher at the Congregational Church for over sixty years

worshipper at this church. In his early years he was amongst the fifty to sixty children who went to this Sunday School. One of the most enjoyable days was the Sunday School summer outing. Mr. Norris, the village carrier, farmer George Brown and many others lent their horses and carts to take the children to Kingley Vale – they sang all the way there and all the way back. A lovely tea was brought along by the mothers for the occasion. There were also the Christmas parties when every

United Reformed Church, while the former schoolroom is now the URC hall available for hire to anyone who wishes to do so. During the war years, table tennis was played regularly in this hall by villagers and servicemen stationed in the area.

In the early 20th century, a need was found for a chapel in Broadbridge at the northern end of the village, so in 1907 a chapel was opened in Gifford Road by Mrs. Duffield, whose husband, a builder, had been a major money raiser. This small chapel was closed in 1954 owing to lack of support and the building is now a private house.

Latterly the Fishermen's Chapel had not had a resident minister, services being conducted by lay readers or visiting ministers to a dwindling congregation. In 2005 the chapel was closed.

The foundation stone of the new Roman Catholic Church of the Assumption of Our Lady was laid in 1967 and completed in 1973 as a daughter church of St. Richards in Chichester. Here a large congregation attend Mass every Sunday and on Feasts of Obligation. It should be appreciated that Bosham Parish Church, until the dissolution of the monasteries, was a Roman Catholic place of worship. With the introduction of the Church of England under Henry VIII, the Roman Catholics had no place of their own in Bosham for about four hundred years until in 1954 a small hut was erected on Fair Field. This field was where, for many years the annual fair and parish church Sunday School Treat had been held in May. The land for this hut had been purchased with the money from the sale of Pearce's Cottage in Taylors Lane, left to the Roman Catholic church by Miss Joanna Preece who died in 1947. In the early 1960s, the hut was condemned so money was raised to build a proper church. In 1981, the church was licensed for marriages, the first one being that of Charles and Susan Clutterbuck, whose family had had a nursery garden for many years in the area now known as Windmill Fields.

There is also today an association, Meeting Point which unites all three congregations, Anglican, Roman Catholic and United Reformed Churches. It was started in 1967 and now holds regular meetings throughout the year in various homes around the village in order to maintain the association's character as being inter-denominational.

The Roman Catholic Church in Fairfield Road, built in 1974

Left: Queen Mary, consort of King George V, visiting Bosham on August 2nd, 1923. To the left is Henry Henshall, churchwarden and artist. His drawings illustrated Kenneth MacDermott's book 'Bosham Church; its History & Antiquities.

Below: Queen Elizabeth, consort of King George VI, later much loved as the Queen Mother, arriving in Bosham on December 9th, 1939.
On the Queen's left, is Mrs Figg in Guider uniform (Girl Guides).

Picture reproduced by courtesy of the Chichester Observer.

CHAPTER 5

Church Visitors

by Sheila Barton August 2001

There must be very few people who come to Bosham and do not visit its beautiful Saxon church. A Visitors' Book in which people can give their names, addresses and make comments has enabled us to estimate that more than 50,000 visitors cross its threshold each year from at least sixty different countries. In probably the earliest Visitors' Book, a heavy leather-bound one given by Mr. E. Howard Wilkins in 1915, was recorded on 2nd August 1923 the signature of H.M. Queen Mary, consort of King George Vth . On December 9th 1939, H.M. Queen Elizabeth, consort of King George VIth signed the Visitors' Book.

Many come on return visits, for anniversaries and to look up family connections. The English language is stretched to its limits as people find adjectives to express their feelings. The church is mysterious, beautiful, delightful, enchanting, celestial, cold, splendid, inspiring, amazing, welcoming, living, creepy, unique, serene, wonderful, spectacular, breathtaking, friendly, spiritual, holy and a balm to the soul - to quote but

The Bosham Viol, now in the Boston Museum of Fine Arts, U.S.A. It was used to lead the congregation in hymn singing until about 1907 when an organ was installed

some of the words used.

There are often comments on the lovely flowers, how well the church is cared for, the wheelchair entrance, and the fact that the building remains open.

Most overseas visitors come from Australia, the USA, Canada, Germany and France with many others from Japan and the countries of Eastern Europe. Perhaps least expected were visitors from Antigua, Bulgaria, Bahrain, China, the Czech Republic, Ethiopia, Guinea, Israel, India, Jamaica, Korea, Mauritius, Malaysia, Niger, Peru, Qatar, Romania, Saudi Arabia, Thailand, USSR, Uruguay, Venezuela and Zimbabwe.

More and more comments are written in a language or even a script we are unable to read! There are visitors of all faiths or none. A Thai Buddhist recently wrote that he 'found peace here' and a couple from Shiraz in Iran said it was their first visit to a church. Mr. Long had been a chorister here in 1922, while Patricia Fitall (née Ede, an old Bosham family) from Fareham said she was christened, confirmed and married here. Peter and Rona Hine from Australia wrote that he lived here until he was nine.

(E.J. and L.F. Hine ran a grocers' shop for many years at the corner of the High St. and Bosham Lane. The shop was rebuilt in 1947 and is now a café.) M. McCall from the Netherlands 'had wonderful memories of my grandfather Rev. Bransby Jones' (Vicar of Bosham 1949-62). In 2001 Bob & Su Walton from Australia wrote '30 years ago today we tied the knot here at this beautiful church'. But Nigel and Rosemary Combes from South Africa did better still, celebrating many events writing 'A peaceful return to Bosham. Baptised, confirmed and married in the church... was a server and bell ringer and two sons were christened here'.

The copy of a section of the Bayeux Tapestry which includes Bosham church is frequently commented upon, as are other special items in the church. We were asked if the picture of a early type of viol was a fake and our subsequent research found that it was a photo of an instrument played by a man in the Bosham church band in 1844 and which is now in the Museum of Fine Arts in the USA. Another visitor was intrigued by the double-headed eagle on the back of a beautiful chair (since stolen). Surprisingly, notice boards are read and commented on, as is the 'glorious east window'. The crypt comes in for comment too and someone wrote 'at the declaration of war [1939] I was here and took refuge in the crypt from a [false] air raid alarm'.

Whenever there is an influx of visitors from a particular country we usually find that Bosham has been featured on television. This recently happened in Poland and Canada when someone wrote that she had seen the vicar and Bosham on TV only a few weeks previously and now she was here in reality. 'May you always be able to leave your door open without fear of damage so that we may sit and be at peace' expressed the feelings of many who thanked us for this. But that door has to be closed sometime as a lady from New Zealand found out when she was nearly locked in at dusk one day! Her cry was heard and she even found enough time and daylight to write 'Loved the church but not so keen about being locked in for the night'.

In the Parish Magazine of August 1902, the then vicar Kenneth MacDermott, wrote 'Our Visitor's Book is fast becoming a most interesting volume, and it affords striking evidence of the fame of Bosham Church...' Two years later, in the magazine of November 1904, the vicar noted that during the previous twelve months no less than 1,316 people wrote their names in the Visitor's Book - an average of four a day throughout the year. The countries that were represented in that earlier book are, surprisingly, almost identical to those that are inscribed in the book today - people came from as far away as Australia, New Zealand, Johannesburg and Ceylon (now Sri Lanka).
The great difference is that today's visitors from far away places have flown here in a few hours whilst those of 1904 would have taken weeks by ship to reach these shores.

It is certainly clear that our lovely church is more than an historic symbol. It provides a variety of experiences and gives so much to so many in different ways. One person wrote *'if inner peace can ever be found, this is the place to start looking'*.

The words on a gravestone in Bosham churchyard:-
In Memory of Thomas, son of Richard Ann Burrow, Master of the sloop 'Two Brothers', who by the breaking of the horse (the bobstay) fell into the sea and was drowned on
October13th 1750, aged 27 years.
The Boreas storms and Neptune's wave
Have tos'd me to and fro
Yet I at length by God's decree
Am harboured here below.
Where at anchor here I lay
With many of our fleet
Yet once again I shall set sail
My Saviour Christ to meet.
In 1750 Bosham was a home for smugglers who are thought to have stored their contraband in the crypt of the church. After the death of her skipper, the Two Brothers *was pursued by customs officers, ran aground on Plymouth breakwater and was wrecked.*

An aerial reconstruction of what the village and quay might have looked like in 1066
(John Pollock)

CHAPTER 6

Following 1066

With the Norman invasion of England, life changed considerably, particularly for the old Saxon aristocracy and the landowners. William had no doubt promised his Norman noblemen that if they supported him with men and materials in his invasion of England, he would reward them handsomely. So most of the English noblemen were stripped of their lands and properties which were then given to William's favourite Norman knights. Although a few of the old laws and ways of administration of the Saxons were retained, a new form of government came to this country based on Norman laws, with Norman French the language of the ruling classes. It was not until 1362 that the language of the English Parliament changed from French to English. There was some continuity before and after William's coronation as there had been some Norman influence in the country prior to the invasion. Edward the Confessor, his childhood spent in Normandy, had filled his court with his Norman friends. Harold II had been Lord of the secular Manor of Bosham, for Edward the Confessor had given the church and the western half of the manor to his Chaplain, Osbern FitzOsbern. As Harold had been crowned king, Bosham was deemed a royal manor, the only one in Sussex. So William lost no time in claiming his lawful possession .

According to the Domesday Book, the register of land, men and materials which was compiled for taxation purposes, Bosham was one of the wealthiest manors in England. Included in the king's part of the manor were fifty six hides of land (about 2,000 acres) with eight mills and two fisheries. There were also eleven sites in Chichester which belonged to this half of the manor. Bishop Osbern, in his half, owned the church as well as one hundred and twelve hides (4000 acres), three mills, a salt house and a host of other items. The church at Thorney Island with a small amount of land was also owned by Bishop Osbern. Before 1066, the whole manor was worth £300, after 1066 only £50, while the clerics held the tithe of the church valued at forty shillings (£2). The mills to which reference is made were probably two at Fishbourne, (a tidal seawater one and a freshwater one) Northbrook, West Ashling, Ratham, Broadbridge, Bosham Quay and Cut Mill. While some of the buildings are still standing in various stages of ruin or repair, none of them is operating as a mill today.

Sussex was to play an important part in the events that followed 1066 for its ports were used as the passageway between England and Normandy. The

41

new administration originally divided Sussex into five rapes, one of which was Chichester, given by William to Roger de Montgomery, his son-in-law and one of his favourite knights, who he created Earl of Arundel in 1067. Each Sussex rape was a north-south strip of land from the northern Sussex border to the coast and each had a castle and a port. In the Chichester Rape, the castle was in Priory Park, Chichester, while the quays at Bosham and Dell Quay were the ports.

However Bosham harbour was virtually decommissioned after Henry I (reigned 1100-35) established Portsmouth and Porchester as ports when the new deep draft sailing vessels were built. Fourteenth-century French pirates took a serious toll of English shipping in the Channel resulting in reduced exports from areas like Chichester Harbour. Nevertheless exports of raw wool continued as well as salt, though the exportation of the latter declined after 1287 when a hurricane seriously damaged the salt pans: salt then had to be imported Towards the end of this period records show that ale was both imported and exported to Normandy; exports also included large quantities of herrings, wheat and oats. Under James II (reigned 1685–88) all goods from foreign parts for the city of Chichester had to go through customs at the port of Dell Quay. In 1671, one merchant reported that the channel to Dell Quay was so shallow that no vessel which drew over nine feet could reach the port except at high spring tides. There is evidence that there was a small Customs Post on Lighters' Field, Bosham

The goods from a barge being unloaded into carts at the Quay in the early part of the 20th century

Hoe, where goods could clear customs and then be transferred either to lighters to be towed up the harbour to Dell Quay or loaded into carts to be taken by land to Chichester. Around 1800, as well as Bosham having a deeper water channel, the tolls at Bosham Quay were lower than those at Dell Quay. In 1799 tolls at Bosham Quay amounted to £40, a year later only £37. In 1851 the Quay was leased to John Martin for twelve months for £20, so it would appear that the profits from the tolls would not have made him a rich man! In 1927, The Lord of the Manor, Viscount Elveden carried out improvements to the Quay. This included raising the height and strengthening the wall of the Quay as well as improving berthing accommodation. As a result of these improvements, vessels of over 500 tons could dock alongside. In January 1927, the Osca from Alderney, a steamer of 550 tons, discharged a cargo of granite chippings. Bosham had blossomed into quite a little port, rivalling Dell Quay.

Each rape was divided into hundreds; this form of land division with its military, judicial and administrative functions, had developed under the Saxons and had been retained by the Normans. It is recorded that King William gave Bosham to William Fitzarthur for a rent of £42 a year. The Hundred of Bosham was first mentioned in 1248; before that Bosham, being in the King's hands, was probably extra-hundredal. From then on the Lordship of the hundred descended through the centuries with the Manor of Bosham. A Hundred was presided over by a reeve who was responsible for maintaining peace in the district and supporting the king in time of war. It is recorded that the Lords of the Manors around Chichester Harbour found difficulty in getting men to answer any call to arms after the month of August when the mackerel fishing season started, as it was essential for the fish to be caught and salted down for winter food. The reeve had to hold regular meetings which had to be free and fair. They were usually held in the open air, thereby showing no favouritism to anyone. The hundred was in turn divided into hides, originally designated as the amount of land one man could cultivate in one year using one plough. This 'hide' could vary in size according to the type of soil or land – it could be anything from sixty to one hundred and eighty acres in size. At the annual Courts of the Hundred the tithing men, later known as the Constable and Deputy Constable, once a year presented their small dues and were given a good dinner, often an oyster feast by the Lord. In Berkeley Castle the Bosham records for between January 1673 to July 1674 under 'Payments made of the Lord Berkeley' there are invoices 'Paid for barroll [barrel] and two hundred oysters 5/6d.'(25p.), 'Paid to the widow Gauntlett for a 'dynnor' [dinner] for the tenants 15/-(75p.) The last of these magnificent feasts of the annual Court of the Hundred was held in 1914.

In 1615 a protest was made by the Lord of the Manor, Lady Elizabeth Berkeley, widow for twenty-four years of Sir Thomas Berkeley, as she considered

The pound from which stray animals could only be released by the payment of a fine.
The shadow of the Swan Inn's chimney can be seen on the left of the picture

that she was not receiving adequate rents from her properties. She descended on Bosham, with John Smythe, her Steward, to meet her tenants. A very efficient business woman, her attempts to raise the revenue from her estates met with little success. There followed endless court cases brought by Lady Berkeley against twenty or more of her chief copyholders. However the Lady Elizabeth went too far, the tenants felt their duties too onerous so a Chancery decision re-established the terms of what became known as the 'Bosham Bible', which restored to the tenants their former claims and customs.

Every Michelmas the Court elections were held when the tenants of the manor elected three officers: the chamberlain, who collected the chief rents, the hayward who gathered copyhold rents (a form of tenancy) and the reeve who acted for the other two in their absence and was often a tenant himself. The reeve, as well as his other duties, also had to ensure that all the fences were in order to prevent any cattle straying. Any cattle that did were put into a 'pound' – one of these was opposite The Swan where there is now a roundabout on the A259 road.

The Court Baron whose duties were to enforce the customs of the manor, met three times a year and consisted of two or three freeholders who had to preside over the various rights and duties of the Lord and his tenants. All tenants of the Lord of the Manor had to attend these Courts – the penalty for non-attendance is unknown but was reportedly severe. Courts Baron for the Manor of Chidham pertaining to properties in the Parish of Bosham are known to have been held in the Anchor in the 19th century.

The Steward of the Manor, usually a

44

The church reflected in the millpond, pictured in 1924. To the right of the church is Mill House, in whose grounds the mill pond (now silted up) lies

lawyer, was the Lord of the Manor's local representative. He was also Admiral of the Seas adjoining the manor and the collector of wrecks; he became known as the Admiral of Bosham and when the regattas took place in Bosham he presided in this official capacity in full dress uniform. It is said that when acting in this role he took precedence over naval admirals while within Bosham waters. Henry Blandford was the last Steward known to have fulfilled this duty at the Bosham Sailing Club's annual regatta in 1951.

Another appointment was that of a Coroner for the Manor and Hundred of Bosham – this appointment also went back to an ancient charter and the holder of this office did not have to be either a qualified lawyer or a doctor. By tradition for many years this role was held by a member of the Cheeseman family. In 1930 Barwell Cheesman had held this appointment for some 35 years - but in 1937 Bosham was brought into the Chichester district by an order under the Coroners (Amendment) Act of 1926 and the local tradition ended.

In 1121 Roger de Montgomery granted Bosham permission to hold six annual fairs – as Arundel at the time was only permitted three, it can be said that Bosham was more important than Arundel in that year. A hundred years later in 1217 the Lord of the Manor, William Marshall, obtained a licence from King Henry III (reigned 1216–72) to hold a weekly market on Thursdays. The Manor courts were always held on market day. In 1637 John Smythe, Steward of Earl Berkeley, reported that this market was not being very well supported!

From William Fitzarthur, the Manor

passed to the Earl of Pembroke, then to the Earls of Norfolk, one of whose daughters married Lord Mowbray and again, through marriage, it passed to William Berkeley (1426–91) 2nd Baron and 1st Earl Berkeley. Thus began 400 years of the Berkeley family being Lords of the Manor and Hundred of Bosham. It was nearly four hundred years before a Berkeley Lord of the Manor was to live here – during those years, the Stewards administered the Manor on behalf of the Lords of the Manor who usually resided in Berkeley Castle in Gloucestershire.

In 1548 after the dissolution of the college, when Richard Sackville took over the estates of the college of canons, the tithes passed to Lay Rectors (Improprietors) who lived at Rectory Farm. The tithes, which amounted to a tenth of all agricultural produce, were kept in the tithe barn of the farm. At that time the tithings held by the Berkeleys were Bosham, Broadbridge, Creed, Walton, Southwood, Hooke and Old Fishbourne. There were also the subsidiary manors of Funtington with East and West Ashling, Thorney Island and Buckfold, a farm near Petworth. The Bishop of Chichester's Prebends (a stipend granted to a member of a cathedral chapter for his support) were Bosham Parochial, Walton, Southwood, Chidham, Westbrook and Appledram. In 1836 this tithing tax was reformed and land owners had to pay in cash rather than in kind. Tithes throughout the country had all been abolished by 1936, probably earlier in the case of Bosham, for in 1932 the 17th century barn at Rectory Farm was demolished and the tiles used to re-roof Herstmonceux Castle in East Sussex.

The 17th century tithe barn at Rectory Farm.

Water mills were first introduced by the Romans who invented the gears which drove the wheels and it is they who may have built the first mills in this area. The first record of a mill in Sussex was in 1186. There were five water mills on the Bosham stream: Northbrook, the first record of which was in 1318 and ceased operation in 1913, West Ashling, a paper mill which also supported a windmill built on the

46

The ruins of Broadbridge Mill, all of which were demolished in 1989. The whole of this area is now a housing estate

top of the building which closed in 1900. Ratham Mill's first recorded operation was in 1600, while the mill on Bosham Quay was in operation in 1325 but was almost certainly working before 1066. In 1582 an indenture granted a lease of twenty-one years from Lord Henry, 7th Baron Berkeley, and his wife, Lady Katharine, to William Trymlett and John Manser in respect of two 'mylls' under one roof comprising one wheat mill and one 'malte' mill together with all necessary furniture. This almost certainly referred to the mill on the Quay, for that was a double mill. In 1601 a similar lease was granted by Lord Henry Berkeley and his son, Thomas, to John Curtiss for twenty one years for £11 per annum to include five fish ponds. There was a large mill pond behind the Mill House off Quay Meadow which was fed by water from the brook. The last miller at the Quay mill was George Brown who ground animal feed until about 1925. This mill finally closed in 1936. His son continued this business with an electric mill in a brick building that was next to the barn that used to stand on the corner of Bosham Lane opposite the then Congregational Church. This electric mill was closed in 1954. Finally there was Broadbridge Mill, where Roman bricks have been found, the first record of which was in 1361 and described as a water powered mill. From 1851 until 1910, the mill was operated by the Gatehouse family. In 1881 Broadbridge Mill was described as being steam and water powered. In 1910 Samuel Gatehouse, registered as a corn merchant, purchased the freehold of the mill from the Lord of the Manor. In 1918 he sold it and it continued to operate under the ownership of William Brignall until 1922. There are the names of a number of members of the Gatehouse family recorded on the 1st World War memorial both in the church and on the War Memorial on Quay Meadow. This mill was totally destroyed in 1989 and there is now a housing estate on the site There was also Cut

47

Mill, which was operating until about 1918/19, the last miller being Amos Wakeford's father. It is now a private house with the wheel still in situ.

In 1665 thousands died in London of the Great Plague. The story goes that in that year a stranger arrived in Chichester and spent the night in a local inn. In the morning he was found dead in bed and the state of his body suggested he had died of the plague. In the same year there is a recorded death of a man in a local hostelry but as parish registry entries of the time did not give cause of death, it is difficult to be sure of what the man died. But it is recorded that on 10th February, 1665, Frances Jaspar, a stranger, was buried at St. Andrews, Oxmarket in Chichester. Thus the story that has come down through the generations is that the Mayor of Chichester, on learning of the death of this one man, immediately ordered that, in order to prevent the spreading of the plague locally, all the gates of the city were to be locked and no one was to be allowed to enter or leave. Notices were placed on the outside of the gates of the city asking people to bring food to the entrances otherwise the inhabitants would starve. The people of Bosham responded to this plea for help and during the night brought food, including fish, to the gates of the city where the townsfolk placed the required amount of money in buckets of water – the only form of disinfectant that was known in those days. In gratitude thereafter, the men of Bosham were permitted to sell their goods in Chichester free of hawkers' licences

There was a Pest House in Bosham outside the village on the south side of the main road between the Swan Inn and Cut Mill, just two rooms of a thatched cottage that stood there. Smallpox was the great scourge of the time and anyone thought to be suffering from this or any other infectious disease was removed to the Pest House. From the 16th to the 18th centuries malaria was a problem in the marsh lands of villages like Bosham but this had largely disappeared by the early 20th century as a result of wholesale marshland drainage schemes. By then, quinine had been discovered as a cure for malaria but would have been available only to those who could afford to buy the drug.

It was not until 1800 that there was a daily coach service between Chichester and Portsmouth, the Swan Inn on the road then called Turnpike Road now the A259, being one of the stops for the coaches. According to the posters advertising the service, The Defiance ran daily from Brighton to the George Hotel in Portsmouth, the return

The Swan Inn in about 1903

The Plague in Chichester – and the help given by the People of Bosham

There have been many accounts of various plagues which have affected some of the local population. Many writers have given differing accounts in books which have been written on Chichester and which include references as to how the people of Bosham fed the citizens of Chichester during a plague. But which plague and in what year?

In the years 1563 and 1608 there were major outbreaks of the plague in Chichester but none in Bosham. John Smyth's History of the Manor of Bosham *written in 1637 makes no mention of any privileges granted to the people of Bosham in Chichester, so one can rule out the two earlier outbreaks in Chichester as being the origin of the story.*

C. J. Longcroft in his book Bosham *printed 1867 gives a long description of how the plague attacked the City of Chichester and many thousands died. He goes on to give a long description of how the people of Bosham brought 'carts laden with meat and grain, with poultry and vegetables to the smitten city! A similar account of the event is give in J. Low Warren's* Chichester: Past and Present *(1901). However Hay's* History of Chichester *(1804) makes no mention of such an incident, although he does include a note on Bosham.*

Leslie Keating in The Book of Chichester *(1979) writes '… it is said that free-roaming lepers placed money in a bowl of vinegar to pay for food left there for them by the townsfolk. The same is said to have been done at the Westgate (Chichester) during the Black Death plague in the 14th century, when villagers from Bosham provisioned the stricken city.'*

Roy Morgan in his book Chichester: a Documentary History *(1992) writes 'The great plague of 1665 was brought to the city by a traveller from London. It spread so rapidly that the Mayor decided to close the city. Near starvation resulted from this* cordon sanitaire *until relief was provided by the people of Bosham who brought food and left it outside the West Gate and collected their money from within buckets of water'.*

In Philip MacDougal's book The Story of Chichester *(2004) 'Potentially more serious was the arrival of plague in 1665' and goes on to say that there were a number of deaths in Chichester that year. But there are no records of any large numbers of deaths in the city that year. There are six recorded burials in St. Peter the Great Registers, Chichester, between October and December 1666 which could be attributed to the plague. There is an account in the Quarter Sessions roll of January 1667 of a tax raised from all the parishes within five miles of Chichester, 'for the relief of the poor within the said city by reason of the infections of the plague there.'*

Mrs. Purser (née Layzell) told of how her grandfather, who was one of the bakers in Bosham operating from the house now called Loafers in Bosham Lane, was allowed to sell his bread in Chichester free of any local taxes because he was descended from one of those who had fed the people of Chichester during the plague. This suggests that the Bosham tradesmen did enjoy some privileges in Chichester markets, which may have been awarded following a plague incident.

journey leaving the George at 9 am. Bookings had to be made at the Dolphin Hotel in Chichester from where coaches also went to the City of London and Piccadilly, as well other towns such as Lewes, Eastbourne and Dover. The London daily papers were available for purchase at the booking offices, so the advertisements read! The era of the stagecoach only lasted fifty years. Before that the traveller went by horse, changing horses every few miles where there was a suitable inn to do so.

A journey from Chichester to London would have taken about ten hours, if there were no problems, at a cost of about £1; this was two months wages for a working man so only the wealthy could consider this form of transport. Goods would have been taken by pack horses or stage-wagons with a canvas top and drawn by four to six horses (like the covered wagons seen in the American wild west films). This form of transport was also used by the less wealthy travellers - lengthy but cheap

Life changed quite considerably for the people of Bosham with the arrival of the railway - Bosham Station was opened for traffic on 15th March, 1847. From then on it was possible to get goods to London in one day. Instead of walking to Chichester, foodstuffs for any local market could be loaded on to a wheelbarrow and placed in the goods van of the train for the merchandise to be sold anywhere between Chichester and Portsmouth. The oyster trade took on a new lease of life with the ability to get the molluscs to London in one day. From being an isolated self-contained little coastal village with little more available than what was in the small local shops or was brought around by itinerant travelling salesmen, suddenly all manner of goods were obtainable from shops in towns many miles away. Many more railway lines were opened at the end of the second half of the 19th century so one could travel from Bosham to Midhurst, Petersfield, Petworth and Pulborough –

the connections were not always easy so it was seldom possible to do the return journey in one day. The rail fare to Chichester was 3d return - about one penny in today's money.

In 1810 Frederick Augustus, the 5th Earl Berkeley, died leaving seven illegitimate children and a further six legitimate ones born after Frederick's marriage to the mother of all his children, Mary Cole an innkeepers daughter. After his death his affairs became a lawyer's nightmare, with only the legitmate children able to inherit the titles but land and property left to each of his, by then, nine surviving children. In his will of some eighty pages, he left the Manor of Bosham to his second natural son, Maurice Frederick Fitzhardinge, who was later created Ist Baron Fitzhardinge. He married in 1823 Charlotte, daughter of the 4th Duke of Richmond of Goodwood, who died of cholera in 1833, leaving four children. Maurice died in 1867 and the manor and the title went to his second son, Charles

Station Road in about the 1920s, with the station in the background and shops on the right.

51

Paget, 3rd Baron Fitzhardinge. Charles, who was childless, on inheriting Berkeley Castle in 1896, sold two years later, the life interest of the Manor of Bosham to his nephew, Edric Frederick, 3rd Baron Gifford. Edric was one of the twelve or thirteen children of Charles' sister, Lady Frederica Charlotte, who in 1845 had married Robert Francis the 2nd Baron. On Edric's death in 1911, the Manor passed to his wife Sophie and then in 1916 to Edric's brother Edgar who had become the 4th Baron. In 1919 Edgar sold off the Manor and all the remaining Berkeley lands in Bosham. Thus ended four hundred years of ownership of the Lordship of the Manor and Hundred of Bosham by the Berkeley family. (See Chapters 11 and 12).

In 1901 Lord Edric sued the Mayor, aldermen and citizens of Chichester for damages caused by faulty sewerage, the pipes for which had been installed in 1893. This resulted in Chichester's sewage emptying into Fishbourne Creek, spoiling fish stocks and producing bad smells. The Court ruled that the apparatus had inadequate capacity and found in the baron's favour. It was thought the case was brought to prove that the Lord of the Manor had the ownership of the mud around the Bosham peninsula.

Following the Law of Property Act 1925 the Manorial Courts Leet and Baron ceased and manorial rights sold to the tenants. The last recorded Court, attended by the Lady of the Manor, Sophie, widow of the 3rd Baron Gifford, was held in the Berkeley Arms on 21st September 1911. There may have been later Courts held but there is no evidence left as all the Berkeley files on Bosham were destroyed by a bomb on the Gifford's solicitors' offices, Raper's, in Chichester during the 2nd World War .

In 1919, Albert Eadie, a Birmingham bicycle manufacturer and inventor of many patented bicycle fittings, bought the Lordship and Hundred of the Manor of Bosham. One gets the impression that Mr. Eadie did not meet with the approval of the locals, for as a start, he had no title! He appeared very magnanimous in offering pieces of land for a W.I. hall and a football ground, only to produce large accounts for unknown legal fees before agreeing to hand over the deeds for such land. So these gestures came to naught. In 1925 the 2nd Earl Iveagh (of the Guinness family) purchased the Manor. He loved Bosham dearly and was very generous in his care of the village. He gave Quay Meadow, the large area between the church and the Quay, with an endowment, to the National Trust. In 1954, he rebuilt the mill on the Quay, utilising much of the old building material to outwardly replicate the historic structure, then

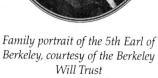

Family portrait of the 5th Earl of Berkeley, courtesy of the Berkeley Will Trust

leased it to the Bosham Sailing Club. After his death in 1963, the Manor passed to his grandson, the 3rd Earl Iveagh, whose father, Lord Elveden, had been killed in action in the 2nd World War. Elveden's name is on the war memorials in the church and on Quay Meadow. In 1976 the Manor and Hundred of Bosham was incorporated into a company, the Burhill Estates Ltd. Today all the Iveagh property in Bosham, mostly around the Quay and Quay Meadow, are incorporated into a new company, the Manor of Bosham Ltd, the shareholders of whom are the descendants of the 2nd Lord Iveagh. Members of the family still occupy their various local properties from time to time.

During the year 1830, the Swing riots broke out when labourers demanded 2/6d (12p) per day, farmers lower rents and the amount of tithes halved. By November of that year, the movement had moved westwards when threshing machines were destroyed at Bosham and Fishbourne. After one incident in Bosham a butcher, bricklayer, brick and stile maker, two sawyers and a carpenter were arrested and imprisoned. It was as a result of these troubles that thirty six special constables were recruited to quell any future riots. The names of the Special Constables were from some of the well known Bosham families such as Cheesman, Bennett, Martin and Frogbrook.

An Act for enclosing lands in the parishes of Bosham and Funtington was passed on 28th May 1821. Public notices were affixed to the outside of the doors of churches and printed in local papers such as the Portsmouth Telegraph, Lewes Journal or any of the

A picture of Quay Meadow in 1947

other current newspapers. A total of eight hundred and thirty acres were enclosed in 1834.

The Local Government Act of 1888 established elected county councils and a further similar act in 1894 empowered any rural area with a population of over three hundred to have a parish council. On 9th January 1895 the first Bosham Parish Council meeting was held which included the parishes of Chidham and Fishbourne. Bosham's Fishbourne, known as Old Fishbourne, consisted at that time of the land west of Salt Hill Road, everything on the east side being part of the City of Chichester. It is thought that the building, The Town Hall, at the end of Bosham Lane, was so named as it was used as the Council Offices for Bosham. Bosham Parish Council originally came under the Westbourne Rural District Council later to be transferred to the Chichester Rural District Council, now just the Chichester District Council. In 1926 Chidham formed its own Parish Council with Major Sydney Beale of Cobnor House, as its first Chairman. The Beale family still own Cobnor House and land around Cobnor Point. In 1939 the Clerk to Chidham Parish Council was paid £5 per year as remuneration for his duties. In January 1988 Fishbourne also broke away from Bosham and formed its own Parish Council, combining the previous Bosham and Chichester areas of Fishbourne into one Council.

At the end of December, 1993, for ten days, Bosham suffered some very severe flooding and the village was almost cut off in every direction when this part of England south of The Downs suffered nearly double its usual average rainfall. As Bosham is largely a flat area

The Trippet. On the right is Town Hall. Once five cottages, it is thought that it acquired it's name by being used as the local council offices at some time

54

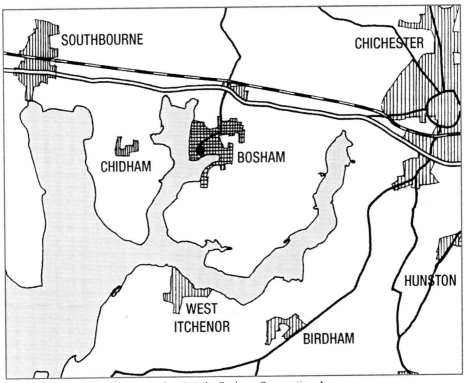

A map showing the Bosham Conseration Area

with clay soil, while the chalk Downs which normally absorb most of the rain, were saturated, the earth simply could not soak up the unusually high amount of rain. The situation was also worse at times of high tides, as the surface water was held back by the sea water.

In the 19th century, floods such as this was taken care of by the farmers who dug open ditches which carried any surplus water down to the harbour. However, over the years, as a result of housing developments and the piping of open ditches, many of which had become blocked with passing time, when there was a higher than average rainfall in the area, the roads everywhere

flooded to a depth of a foot or more. A certain amount of first aid was done by clearing pipes. A similar situation arose in 1998, but luckily another disaster was averted as a result of the clearing of ditches and pipes.

During the thousand years following the Norman Invasion of England, Bosham became an insignificant place in English history – it was just a small fishing village within Chichester Harbour. Except for the period of over one hundred years that the Berkeley family occupied Old Park, there was no great family in residence in a Manor House, who would have had their own private family pews and large memorials in the church, while there were few locals employed in all the facets of running a large estate. This would have influenced the history of Bosham during that millennium. However, In June 1944 Bosham was to come into its own again in the part that it took in what might be called the return invasion, when England invaded Normandy on D-Day. Prior to that day, the whole of Chichester Harbour was filled with small naval vessels of every description while some of the pontoons for the Mulberry Harbours were built or assembled at Bosham. More of that time can be read in the chapter "Recollections of the 20th century".

Bosham is within the Chichester Harbour Conservancy, an area so designated by Act of Parliament in 1971. The whole of the waters of the harbour as well as the land around the shore are managed by a Harbour Master/Manager with a board of management. This board consists of representatives from all the various interests in the harbour as well as members of the County and District Councils of Hampshire and West Sussex. The Manor of Bosham still owns the mud under the water between the middle of all the channels around the Bosham peninsula up to mean high water mark, while most of the shoreline as well as Lighters' Field on Bosham Hoe are Sites of Special Scientific Interest (SSSI). The whole of the harbour is designated an Area of Outstanding Natural Beauty. That area of Bosham bounded by the sea on the west and south sides, on the north by Bosham Lane and to the east by a line south eastwards from Critchfield Road, is within the Bosham Conservation Area. This area is also subject to very strict controls which help to conserve the future of the village, not as a museum but as a thriving area for boating, sailing and pleasure.

The waterfront of Bosham at half tide

1. Street End,
Bosham Lane, with
Gloucester House on left

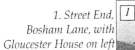

2. Bosham Lane
looking north

3. The Mill, now Bosham Sailing Club

4. Street End at (very!)
high tide

5. Bosham Lane with Millstream
Hotel & Chapel Cottage, the
thatched cottage on left

Today Bosham is an ever-enlarging village. The fishing and boat building industries have gone, the fishing boat moorings are now used for yachts and the shipyards closed. At weekends in the summer the waters heave with the many coloured sails of boats of every size being navigated by those of every age. The region has become a commuter's paradise for those working in an area that stretches from Southampton to Brighton, from Horsham to Bognor, as well as being a popular place for the weekenders, for the tired and retired. The village now has a new role for, with the discovery of the Roman Palace at Fishbourne, it has become a popular tourist attraction with the roads and shore, when tides permit, packed with visitors and their cars. Nevertheless it is a thriving and growing community with activities and clubs catering for everything from badminton to yachting, from gardening to the Women's Institute – in short it is a flourishing society of some three thousand souls.

The waterfront of Bosham village with the downs behind viewed from the Chidham peninsula. On the far right Goodwood Racecourse is tucked into the hills.

CHAPTER 7

Recollections
of the Twentieth Century

The hundred years between 1900 and 2000 must have seen the greatest changes in English village life ever known.

In the Bosham of 1900, like the majority of villages in this country, there would have been few houses with indoor sanitation or running water. Only very few of the larger houses would have had electricity. Of an evening the majority of the families would have sat in oil or candlelit rooms in their small cottages, with little to do except listen to grandfathers' recounting the incidents of the past, some of these learned from their grandfathers. Cool boxes or refrigeration of any kind would have been non-existent, but most houses would have had a marble slab with a net covered container somewhere on the north side of the house where perishable food could be kept for a short time. Laundry was done by hand while many articles would be boiled in the copper – a facility that was also used for heating the water for the weekly bath as well as for boiling puddings, like those eaten at Christmas.

A hundred years on there are few houses without indoor toilets and bathrooms, most of the village is on main drainage, while just about everyone has electricity which enables them to listen to radio or watch television with all the possibilities that that gives. There are few houses without refrigerators and clothes washing machines, nor are there many without a deep freeze of some kind.

The roads of 1900 were gravel, a dust bowl in summer and a muddy quagmire in winter, when the ladies had to lift up their skirts to prevent muddying the hems of their dresses. By 2000 there were few, if any, gravel roads in the village. There were few house owners in the early part of the 20th century. In 1900, landlords charged rents which sound ridiculous today – 2/6d (12.5p) rent per week for a two-up and two-down house in the High Street with no services whatever, not even a well in the garden. But a jug of milk could be bought for one penny. Some of the wealthier tradesmen might own more than the one house in which they lived and would rent out the others.

Between the two world wars, eight council houses (that is local government built and owned) were built in Taylors Lane. These houses had no electricity or indoor sanitation until a few years before the 2nd World War. After the war twelve prefabricated council houses were built in the field where now is Critchfield Road and these were allocated to returning married members of the forces. Rita and Sonner Gilby moved into one of these prefabs and remember feeling that they were living in luxury. As well as having main drainage and a bathroom, each house was fitted with a fridge, a built-in copper, a cooker as well as hot air central heating. The following year permanent council houses were built on the opposite side of Critchfield Road and also in the old brick yard, now Brooks Lane, at Broadbridge, north of the Main Road (A259). The prefabs in Critchfield Road were dismantled in 1961 to be replaced with permanent buildings. The rents for council houses were lower than those in the private sector, for the council rents did not include a profit element as any private landlord would need. So there was always a waiting list for those wishing to acquire a council house.

In the 1980s, in order to encourage home ownership, sitting tenants were allowed to buy the council houses they occupied. For those that did not have the capital available to purchase the house outright, the council provided the tenants with mortgages which were funded by what the tenants had previously paid as the weekly rent. The sale price was dependent upon how long the tenant had occupied that particular house. Nearly all the farms had tied cottages; that is such dwellings could be occupied only by those employed by the farmer – their tenancy ceased when their employment on that particular farm ended.

Main drainage did not come to Bosham until the 1930s. Until then the people of the village had to rely on the privy at the bottom of the garden, the brook or the tides. Eva Purser, grand-daughter of one of the Bosham bakers, remembers that about once a month, the night soil carts arrived to empty the privies. To obliterate the smell, herbs or scent were poured on lumps of sugar and burned. Other people just dug holes at the bottom of the gardens and when the hole became full, another hole was dug and the hut and lavatory seat moved to the new position. For those that lived in the

Jackie Gilby, aged two, daughter of Rita and Sonner Gilby, outside their home, one of the prefabs in Critchfield Road. June 1949

High Street their privy was a hole in the wall of the room facing the sea, to await the arrival of high tide to carry all away. The big houses would have had bathrooms with a cesspit or septic tank in the garden into which the effluent went. These tanks too needed emptying at regular intervals.

As there is no natural water course into that part of Bosham around the church, an area we know the Romans occupied, it must have been they who built the aqueduct, or brook, which provided the villagers with a water supply. For those whose houses were near enough to the brook to be able to dip their buckets into the running water (and into which they could also tip their spoil) life was comparatively easy. For others it meant collecting buckets of water from the dip holes of which there were three down Bosham Lane. The remains of one, now with a man hole cover, can be seen at the south-east corner of the Manor House grounds alongside Bosham Walk. On the west side of the gardens of the Manor, the brook runs some few feet higher than the lawns; water from the brook also runs round three quarters of the Manor House grounds.

For some inexplicable reason, the locals collected their drinking water only from the brook at the corner by Brook House; the stone on which the water collectors stood can still be seen under the water just by the bridge - if the brook is not too muddy. Why the water here should be considered any different to that in the dip holes cannot be imagined, for it came from the same source and would have had the same

An 1888 etching of the brook. On the left is Brook House with the mill in the background.
It was here that the villagers obtained their drinking water

61

additions on its route from Ratham Mill. In fact Humphrey Selwyn Lloyd in his diaries wrote that, not surprisingly, typhoid was very prevalent when he came first to Bosham in 1900.

At the Manor House, Duke, the gardener, every morning at 7 a.m. took twenty minutes to pump the water for the household's daily use. Some remember that the water for drinking was boiled and then filtered. Rosie Frogbrook recalls how, every so often, the brook would overflow in the area where there is now the Bosham Sailing Club dinghy park. Watercress grew in abundance and the children were sent there after school to pick some for their tea. However, during the first week of June each year, the water supplying the brook was cut off somewhere near West Ashling, the three mills were closed while the banks of the

James Duke the gardener in the grounds of the Manor House in the early 1900s

brook were cleaned, each owner or farmer being responsible for his own section of the brook. Those households who fetched their water from the brook, filled every available container to store enough water to last that week. The water was so precious that it was never thrown away until it was really dirty. There were many houses in Bosham that had wells, but they were usually only those some way from the sea to avoid the risk of pollution by salt water.

Eva Purser, who lived some of her early life in 3 Adelaide Terrace, remembers that they had their own well, as did the neighbouring houses. In their house, there was a small room off the stairs where the family had their hip baths. Another remembers her mother insisting upon a dollop of Izal, being put in the bath. Izal was a popular disinfectant of the time not unlike today's Jeyes Fluid. Gertrude Arnell, born in 1888 in Mariners' Terrace, wrote that in her early childhood, water was collected from a ditch at the back of the cottages. When the family moved to Harbour Cottages, the water was collected from the brook by Brook House – at the weekends their father did it, but during the week she and her sister did the fetching after school, 'a bucket each and a bath carried between us'. Each member of the family had one bath a week – usually on Saturday night. The water was heated in the copper (in which the clothes were boiled on Mondays), when the tin bath was filled with hot water and placed in front of the kitchen stove.

Selwyn Lloyd in the early years of the century did everything in his power to get mains water – he approached the Medical Officer of Health for the District, who was in Brighton, as well as the Rural District and Parish Councils with little effect. The reason was that the local farmers and cottage owners were terrified that it would result in an increase in their rates! Finally he approached the President of the Local Government board in London, who applied pressure to the County Council. As a result in 1910 water came to the centre of the village and typhoid became unknown. Outlying areas like Smugglers Lane and Bosham Hoe did not get a mains water supply until the early 1930s. Delling Lane did not get their supply until 1948 but there were few houses in this area until after the 2nd World War.

Margaret Coward, with her sister Edie, who in later years, were to run the Country Stores in Bosham Lane, a few doors south of the then Congregational Church, recalls life as a child at Church Farm in Old Park Lane in the early part of the century. While her father worked in the fields, the girls helped their mother preserve for winter use all that their father grew: carrots, onions, turnips, swedes, strawberries, raspberries, followed in the autumn by apples and blackberries, mushrooms and medlars. There was lovely fresh milk almost straight from the cow, from which came their cream and butter, and plenty of brown eggs from the hens. Trixie Balchin, who lived on Gosportside (see picture on Page 74), daughter of Harry John Apps (a fisherman in winter, a yacht hand in summer) recalled that either she or her sister had to collect a quart of milk in a round tin can from farmer Brown's dairy at Mill House, Quay Meadow. They also had to collect the beer for their father's tea from the

The young Coward children helping to drive the cows home at Church Farm, Old Park Lane

Off Licence, Benbow on Gosportside (the house now called Benbow), run by George Apps, on their way home from school. George Apps was quite an artist and in the evening he used to sit in an armchair by the fire with a clay pipe in his mouth and draw big birds on cardboard, which he then hung on the walls of the pub.

In winter evenings, the thick heavy curtains were drawn, the kitchen range stoked up while the whole family played card or other games. On Saturday nights, father would go along to the 'local' – women, except those of ill-repute, were never seen in pubs in those days.

But Sunday was different, everyone dressed in their best clothes, the children spent the morning learning that day's Collect to be recited at Sunday School in the afternoon. The vicar, Mr. Mitchell, came down from the vicarage, accompanied by his daughter

Minnie, the Sunday School teacher. A pony and trap were hired from Freddie Martin of the Ship Inn for the journey. The vicar took his meals in a private room of the Anchor between the Sunday services. The big talking point of his time was when one of his daughters, Charlotte Sophia, eloped with George Martin, a ship owner and captain and a brother of the two landlords of the Anchor and the Ship. Of all the vicar's six children, she ended up by being the wealthiest. The Rev. Kenneth MacDermott took over from Mr. Mitchell in 1902 and with a younger livelier vicar, the atmosphere in the village became a little more relaxed. The young vicar married soon after his arrival and it was not long before he had a young family.

In 1906, a free lending library was set up in the vicarage 'open to all' which meant non-churchgoers as well – borrowers had to contribute three pence

A picnic party from the village at Kingley Vale in 1914

(1p.) per annum to cover administrative costs. Anyone with books to spare was asked to donate them while the SPCK gave £6 for the library to purchase new stock. When a village hall was built in 1925, cupboards were built for books, stocked from the main library in Chichester and the library was opened for a few hours every week, manned by volunteers. This continued for many years until a mobile library service was started, which now visits the village regularly.

Eva Purser recalls that at the time of the Christmas, Easter and Harvest Festivals, all the young parish church-goers, armed with picnics, went to Kingley Vale up in The Downs in farm carts to pick holly, daffodils, seedheads, greenery and anything else that was available, to decorate the church.

Eva also remembers as a small child, seating herself in one of the front pews of the parish church. A voice from behind startled her 'Now my girl, what do you think you are doing sitting there – that is where you should be' and getting hold of her arm, Mr. Mitchell pushed her into one of the pews at the back of the church. It was a long time before she could be persuaded to go to church again.

Trixie Balchin remembers the winter temperature of the church – it was often barely above freezing – there was an enormous boiler at the back of the building which was stoked with coke, but that did little to heat the church effectively. In the 1950s Tommy Guy, the local village plumber, installed the central heating system – great big black pipes were put in around the

The interior of the church in 1881. On the left of the picture is the old boiler which provided very inadequate heating for the church

church at floor level. It did take the chill off the church on very cold days, but that was about the limit of its heating abilities.

The kitchen ranges in the cottages were fed with wood; sometimes there was coal available, gleaned from the quay after the coal barges had finished unloading. Both Trixie Balchin and Bogia Coombes recall going 'wooding' around the shore to collect enough wood to feed their mothers' kitchen ranges for a week. During the 1st World War, when a lot of ships were sunk, the cargo from the sunken vessels often landed up on the shores around the harbour. Bogia told of how, on one occasion, a number of twelve foot long planks were washed up. When the customs officers got wind of them, they came around to claim the contraband. The boys laid the timber on the shore side of a sea wall and stood on the planks. The boys engaged the officers in conversation – and the officers left empty handed! Another time a number of boxes of butter got washed up and the young lads followed the same procedure. The wood and butter were sold, of course, retaining some of both commodities for themselves! After the harvest each year, the villagers also went gleaning in the fields for corn with which to feed their poultry. Most of the kitchen ranges had only very small ovens which were not big enough to take the Sunday joint. A roasting tin with the meat and peeled potatoe topped with dripping, was taken to the nearest bakery or to anywhere else where there was a large oven. The landlord of the Ship had one such oven opposite his pub. The joint was dropped off on the way to church, to be collected after the service on the way home. It cost tuppence (two old pennies) a joint .

It was a two mile walk to the parish church from Church Farm for the

The tollgate in the 1920s, which was by the church path in the High Street. On the left is the old school house where Rosie Frogbrooke's grandmother was the school mistress

Coward children, the same walk the children did every day to school. They would take something for their lunch – a piece of home-made bread, a chunk of cheese, an apple and perhaps a can of milk from the morning's milking. There were no worries then about the children walking alone to school as there are today.

For a few years, in the early 1920s when Mr. Eadie was the Lord of the Manor, there was a tollgate on the corner by the church in the High Street – it cost one old penny to pass through that gate – 1d less for the church collection!.

Eva Duke, born in 1892 and whose father-in-law was the gardener at the Manor House, wrote how the people of the village made their own entertainment when she was a child. Bosham was a very sociable village: Mrs. Ellen Sheen (née Frogbrook) remembers the men gathering on Sunday mornings at Street End to play marbles waiting for noon when the pubs opened, then going to church with their families at 6.30 in the evening. There was the Sunday School treat with visits to Littlehampton or Bognor as well as the fairs held on May 20th on the fair field – the name remembered in Fairfield Road which runs across the field and where now there is a housing estate.

Lylie Merrett, whose parents ran the Gloucester Inn at Street End recalled how there were concert parties there – groups of men, calling themselves the 'Bonfires' and the 'Bosham Blackbirds' used to entertain the village with the most wonderful singing. They practised regularly in the Gloucester, the magnificent sounds echoing all around School Rithe. It was in the Gloucester that some of the local 'dinners' were held, while Christmas parties took place in the Tap Room of the Anchor.

Humphrey Lloyd and his wife May, who lived in the Manor House, started a concert party on the lines of the "Follies" called the Bosham Pierrots. They performed for two or three years in surrounding villages and towns, raising money for local charities. They made their own drag curtains and hand painted wooden back-of-the-stage scenery.

Humph wrote the music and rehearsed the group in the Manor House. One of the items was when 6'3" ((1.6 m) 'Lanky' Towner dressed up as a gigantic teddy bear and, with his pretty little wife, provided one of the popular hits in the programme. Another star was Mrs. Pitts who sang sentimental songs like 'My Moon' and 'Little Grey Home in the West', while May Lloyd and the Vicar's wife, Mrs. MacDermott, as well as half a dozen others, provided the chorus. When the Pierrots performed in the Chichester Theatre in South Street, the Mayor and Corporation of the city took up the entire front row. When performing in Emsworth, such was its popularity, they had to put on two extra performances.

The Lloyds at the Manor House financed the Coronation festivities for King Edward VII in 1902.

The adults were given beer and stout – some forty gallons of it was consumed that day - as well as ham, beef and bread and butter. The children got through thirty gallons of milk, sixteen plum cakes and thirty other cakes. The fireworks could be seen many miles away in the Solent. Some 1004 people entered the Manor House grounds that evening. At the end of the evening when the workers sought a little bit of food and sustenance after a hard day's work, there was not a scrap of anything, food or drink, left in the house. Gertrude Arnell recollects as a child of thirteen her father, a fisherman, taking his whole family, as well as others from Bosham, out on his vessel, The Nellie, to watch a Naval Review by King Edward VII in Spithead.

Nellie Jellett, who lived in one of the Creed Cottages, Walton Lane, when a young girl in service in the 1920s, used to go with a group of young people to the pictures regularly in Chichester. They walked there along the public footpath across the fields by Strange Hall to Fishbourne and then on to Chichester, to return by train to Bosham station and walk the rest of the way home. The cost of the return rail fare Bosham/Chichester in the early 1900s was 3d (just over 1p)

Ellen Sheen recalls Bonfire Night, the 5th November, when after school the children were taken around the village in farmer Brown's wagon to

The Manor House decorated for the coronation of Edward VII, which was hosted by Humphrey Selwyn Lloyd

GOD BLESS OUR KING & QUEEN
&
GOOD LUCK TO HAPPY BOSHAM

Humphrey Selwyn Lloyd with Kenneth MacDermott's son, at the Dutch fête of 1907 held in the vicarage gardens. The couple in the background are thought to be Mr & Mrs Thomas Apps of the Apps Shipyard

68

1. The Manor House party enjoying their cup of tea whilst watching the regatta of 1901 or '02.
Mrs (Caroline) Selwyn Lloyd (farthest left) has a particularly dashing hat to wear on such an occasion - photograph taken by her husband, Humphrey!

2. Spectators at the Regatta of 1912 in the vessel Excel. This ship was used as the flagship by the Admiral of Bosham at the annual regattas. Pictured are Captain Freddie Woods, the owner of Excel, his wife (née Kate Smart of Smart's Yard) their daughter Dolly, Mr & Mrs Harry Martin & their daughter & Mr Coward later of Coward's Stores

3. The spectators at the 1902 regatta. Note the ice-cream seller on the right

4. Yachts in a regatta in the 1920s

collect coppers (old pennies) for the Guy and for fireworks. They went as far as Old Park, where Lady Gifford, wife of the Lord of the Manor, always gave them something, shouting as they went "Remember, remember, the 5th November'. In the meantime others had organised a large bonfire which was lit about 7.30 and while it was blazing away, everyone sang accompanied by Aunt Mary Batchelor on her concertina. The last of such splendid evenings was in 1913 – the 1st World War must have put paid to such a noisy flaming bonfire evening. Trixie Balchin remembers dressing up with garlands of flowers in her hair and going into Chichester, with a group of others from Bosham, in farm carts to take part in the Bonfire night in Chichester.

Then there were the annual regattas, the first one being in 1907 and directed from The Studio in Shore Road. For many years, the principal organiser of the regattas as well as many other events, was Mr. Murton, one of the village bakers. His shop was in the house formerly called Poplars, now renamed the Old Bakehouse in Bosham Lane. The regattas were not as they are today just for boats, but there were games and competitions in which the whole village took part. Bogia Coombes recollects the boxing booths in Bull's field, opposite the Anchor, and the swings and roundabouts on Quay Meadow. There would be coconut shies and a shooting gallery all held in the area of the High Street and Quay Meadow. There would be the greasy pole event, beauty and ankle competitions and catching the well-greased pig – whoever caught the animal was allowed to keep it.

Henry Blandford in 1951, Steward of the Manor and Admiral of Bosham

The Regatta of 1908 was held under the distinguished patronage of the Duke of Richmond and Gordon, Hon. Lord Gifford, Lord of the Manor, and the Mayor of Chichester. Lady Gifford presented the prizes where, in addition to a cup there might be for that particular event, there was usually a monetary prize - £1 for first, 15/- (75 p) for second and 10/- (50 p) for third. Events included a Ladies Double-handed Rowing Race in Bosham fishing boats – the clothing worn by the ladies had to be vetted by the committee (no short skirts) when the prize for the winner was an umbrella.

One of the most important persons at the Regattas was the Admiral of Bosham, otherwise the Steward of the Manor. He took precedence when royalty entered the parish and when the fleet or any unit of the fleet entered the harbour. In either of these cases, the Admiral of Bosham, dressed in wig, gown and bibs, received the visitors and escorted them to the quay. At regattas he had a salute of eleven guns as he presided in a merchant ship of some sort – during the years prior to the 1st World War it was the 'Excel', a ketch rigged trading vessel. A bunch of holly was attached to the mast head of the chosen vessel and as soon as the Admiral appeared, the salute started. When the Admiral reached the selected vessel, through a megaphone, the Admiral declared the regatta open. As far as is known, the last time this ceremony took place was in 1953 in the year of Queen Elizabeth's II Coronation.

Eva Purser (née Layzell) told of the annual church fetes, started by the young Mr. MacDermott, held in the vicarage gardens in which everyone took part. Walton House was then the vicarage while the former gardens are now covered with greenhouses. The church fêtes lasted many days; excursions were run from Brighton, Portsmouth and Southampton by the railway companies, the band of the Royal Sussex Regiment played and there were many well known visitors like the Duke of Richmond and the Bishop of Chichester. The Swiss Fête in 1904 was held in glorious weather and attracted some 3000 visitors as well as raising £294 for church funds. When the Vicar wanted to raise £2,000 to do some restoration work in the church in 1907, a Dutch Fête was held in the vicarage grounds. The first day was wet and cold but the Lloyd family had brought back some 'Vollendam' clothing (possibly a new insulated material, the latest thing) from Holland and were themselves the warmest people around. Humph ran the tobacco and photograph stall, while Glyn Martin sold some of Dr. Ernest Buckell's photos (148 of them) A photo cost 1/- (5p) if it was just a landscape picture, 2/- (10p) for those with one person and 3/- (15p) for those with more than one person in the picture.

Lloyd also wrote the words for a song 'Bosham by the Sea' sung to the tune of the Eton Boating Song. He had five hundred copies printed, sold the lot and had to have a reprint, which cost £5 including copyright and cover. (The words of the song can be found in Chapter 16 - Songs & Poems)

In the 1950s the dancing group 'Martlet Sword & Morris Men' who regularly visited all the villages around Chichester, came to Bosham. They usually performed outside the pubs – which of course the landlords encouraged for it brought them a great deal of trade. The two pubs in Bosham outside of which they usually performed, were the Swan and the Anchor.

Another popular event was to follow the hunt for which Lady Gifford was the Master of Foxhounds

71

1. Some of the stall holders at the Swiss fête of 1904 (Note the price of teas - 6d (2½p).
2. Ye Olde Englishe Fête of 1912 - the helpers in their mob caps.
3. The Dutch fête viewed from an upstairs window of the vicarage.
4. The scene at the Swiss fête of 7th July 1904.
5. Maypole dancing in front of the Manor House at the Church Fête on 26th July 2002.
6. & 7. The programmes of the Swiss Fête of 1904 and the Church Fête of 26th July 2002

(MFH). Lady Gifford also had a pack of harrier hounds for hunting hares. Lord Leconfield too had a pack of foxhounds at Petworth and they met on occasions at either Old Park or at the Black Boy in Fishbourne, just around the corner from Old Park. There was an annual point-to point held in the grounds of Old Park, when a seating stand was temporarily erected. Lord Gifford was known as the Rat Catching Peer, as he had a pack of thirty rat catching dogs, mostly terriers. He went all over the parish with a crowd of followers, working the hedgerows and the edges of the creek killing rats. His rat catching quotas were reported yearly in the Sporting & Dramatic News" – the year before his death in 1911, his catch was reported to have amounted to twenty five thousand rats.

Bosham was a popular place for artists – Selwyn Lloyd wrote in his diaries of parties coming over from France and groups of them would be seen sitting on stools around the shore painting away. One artist tells of arriving at Bosham station as 'the last rays of the setting sun had died.. .. the grey horse of the Bosham waggonette had come to meet us' and they were transported down to Street End to stay in one of the houses along the shore. Surprisingly today few of these paintings are to be found.

Eva Duke had 1d (one old penny) a week pocket money which she usually spent in the Sweet Shop at the end of the High Street. When she married at the age of twenty one, she and her new husband moved into May Cottage on Shore Road, where the rent was 3/6d (17p) per week and her weekly housekeeping allowance was 15/- (75p.). In the early 1900s James Duke, the gardener at the Manor House,

Above:
Lady Gifford's harrier hounds in front of Old Park House in 1912. Lord Gifford was the Lord of the Manor

Below:
Spectators at Lady Gifford's Point to Point races held in the grounds of Old Park in 1912

earned £1 a week and had the use of a cottage in the Manor House grounds – he did well for at the time a gardener's wages were 15/- (75p today) per week and no house.

Sophia Guy, whose husband was the village plumber, recalled how her father, the carrier for the Heaver family, grew and kept the family in vegetables all the year round. Her mother could only afford to buy meat once a week – the Sunday joint, served cold on Monday (wash day) and the remains minced on Tuesday. On other days her mother bought two pennyworth of bones from the butcher and with every vegetable available from the garden, she produced a wonderful vegetable stew. Mrs. Guy maintained the result was far more tasty as well as being very much more nourishing than anything she had eaten since.

Mrs. Guy had a tubercular hip and wrote of the wonderful care she received from their local doctor as well as the Royal West Sussex Hospital where her hip was operated on – she was cured, though left with a permanent limp. Her father paid the doctor with bags of potatoes or other vegetables. This would have been in addition to the 2/6d (12p.) that the family would have paid annually into the 'panel' – a form of medical insurance.

In the early part of the century, the doctor had a surgery in the house between the Ship and the Anchor – now called 'Before Anchor'. Dr. Buckle was also a great photographer and there are many photos that he has left behind, some taken from the roof of the tower during renovations to the church in 1903. He came out to Bosham in Freddie Martin's (landlord of the Ship) Wagonette which, with the horse, was kept in the stables opposite the Ship. If the doctor was required urgently, the only means of contacting him was to send him a telegram from the Post Office - a telegraph boy would have delivered the message to the doctor's house, the doctor would then need to get some means of transport to reach the sick patient. So it could be two to three

A photograph taken by Dr. Buckle, the local doctor, from the spire of the church when it was being re-roofed in 1903. Across School Rithe is Gosportside, a hamlet which had a shop and a pub

hours before the doctor arrived. Humphrey Selwyn Lloyd, because he had had some medical training, was frequently asked to visit a sick person so that a more accurate picture of their illness could be given when telegraphing the doctor.

Half a century later, the National Health Service had come into being – district nurses, doctors, ambulances and hospitals were available to all and with most people connected to a telephone, help was available in a very short time

In the Parish Magazine of October, 1910, it quotes the rate at which the over 70s could claim an old age pension. Anyone having an annual income of under £21 a year could claim 5/- (25p.) a week pension. The idea today that it would be possible to live on 25 pence a week seems unbelievable. In old age, if one had no family able to look after one, people went to the Workhouse Infirmary at Westbourne which,

according to Humphrey Lloyd when he visited the place in 1920, was a disgrace – cold, bleak and gloomy.

In 1977, Britannia Court, a sheltered housing complex, was built in Taylors Lane by the District Council. This consisted of a number of one and two-roomed self contained flats for the elderly, with Vincent Foote as its first warden. By moving into Britannia Court, a single person, left alone when the family had grown up and left home, would release a three-bedroomed house for occupation by a young family. A far better prospect than that faced by a widow left alone in the early 1900s with only the workhouse in which to end her days

During the 1st World War, when the menfolk went off to fight, the women were left to take over many of the men's jobs. In the Parish Magazine of February, 1916, the women of the village were asked 'to do their bit' by growing vegetables and fruit, helping

Britannia Court in Taylors Lane, a sheltered complex of one and two roomed flats for the elderly, built in 1977

with milking the cows, picking fruit for bottling or to make jam. 'All work done for the farmers will be paid at a fair rate' so the advertisement read.

In 1915, special egg services were held in the Congregational Church and also in the chapel at Broadbridge, when Miss Kate Wells, the superintendent of the local weekly egg collection, was present with her fellow collectors. The three hundred and five eggs collected by members of the two congregations were sent to the egg depot for distribution amongst wounded soldiers

Prior to the arrival of the buses, there was a period when Mr. Norris ran a horse-drawn covered wagon with windows, daily into Chichester. It left Street End, Bosham, at 1 o'clock each afternoon and left the Chichester Cross for the return journey at 4 p.m. It cost 3d (1p) return. On the way to Chichester, the driver detoured around the village to pick up passengers – if you wanted him to call, you put a special coloured card in your window. If you did not want to go yourself, a young lad would do your shopping for you – for a consideration! George Purver also ran a regular carrier service to Bosham, leaving The Eagle Inn in West Street, Chichester, at 3.30 p.m. daily. After the 1st World War, the Carpenters brothers, one of whom lived in Rose Cottage with his wife and family, ran a lorry with seats which took people into Chichester.

There was a story that there was a highwayman at the top of Walton Lane. Lylie Merret remembers how a man used to hide in the hedge on the old turnpike road by the vicarage (now Walton House) and hold up the wagonette and demand money.

Between the two world wars, labour had become more mobile, for the industries that gave them employment were outside the village in places like Portsmouth and Chichester.

The William Pink's waggonette which provided a daily service into Chichester

There were the regular train services from Bosham Station between Portsmouth and Brighton, while in the 1930s the Southdown Bus Company had begun a regular service to Street End from Chichester. A few years before that Southdown had run the No.31 bus which ran a hourly service along the main road, the A27 now the A259, between Portsmouth and Brighton. By the year 2000 there were few people who lived and worked in Bosham.

There was the village midwife who delivered all the babies in the mothers' own homes. At the beginning of the 20th century it was Mrs. Savage. With no official medical training, she brought forth no less than one hundred babies. Moreover, Mrs. Savage insisted, when doing a delivery, on two tots of gin being available, one for the mother-to-be, the other for herself. When she died, a fully trained district nurse/midwife was appointed to the village. In the 1940s and 50s it was the well known Nurse Nixon who lived in Nightingale Cottage, almost opposite the Berkeley Arms in Delling Lane. She must have delivered thousands of babies in her time, for it was not until about the 1960s that mothers went to maternity homes or hospitals for the big event.

For those who 'passed on' there was Mrs. Polly Frogbrook, wife of Captain Mark Frogbrook. She was the village 'layer out' for nearly fifty years. She was proud of having 'laid out' over a hundred members of the Frogbrook family alone and always preserved a small piece of wood from each coffin. For some years she was cook to the Lloyd family when they lived at The Grange, now the Millstream Hotel. A wonderful woman, full of folk lore and superstition and, although she had a large family, when old spent many years in the Chichester Workhouse Infirmary until rescued by Humphrey Selwyn Lloyd. He managed to get members of the Frogbrook family to contribute to a fund which enabled Polly to live in the care of Mrs. Humphreys (no relation) in Chapel Cottage – Mrs. Humphreys was paid £1.10s (£1.50)a week for Polly's keep, while Polly herself was given 2/- (10p) a week pocket money and a bottle of beer a day.

SEPTEMBER 24, 1940
Raider Down at Bosham

At a Sussex town on Saturday afternoon a short but sharp air battle took place overhead.

One German bomber was rocked by A.A. fire before two Spitfires pounced on it's tail. The raider glided round in a semi-circle, eventually crashing at Bosham.

It brushed the roof of the Nunnery, and cleared the roof of a motorbus on the main road by inches, giving the passengers and driver the fright of their lives.

It cleared a railway train by the same narrow margin, and crashed in a meadow. Immediately it was surrounded by a swarm of 30 boys who had been blackberrying in the neighbouring fields.

Without thought for their danger they jumped over the electrified rails to meet four Germans who clambered out of the machine. The airmen were quickly taken into custody by the police.

Little Ernie Burchall, aged five, received a broken arm when struck by a piece of falling A.A. shell while blackberrying four miles away from the scene of the crash.

While visiting the cemetery, Mrs Stamp was startled when another piece of shrapnel fell across her shoulders, and Mr P. Knott, usher at a wedding, was hit in the back by a spent machine gun bullet.

(continues)

In the early part of the century smuggling continued, tobacco and silk being the two principle items, the last known case being in 1905. According to Humphrey Lloyd, local lugsail fishing boats, equipped with false sterns, rendezvoused with 50 - 60 ton scalloping vessels to pick up the contraband five or six miles off the harbour entrance. The tobacco usually came from the Channel Islands where there was no duty. The contraband was landed at different villages around the harbour – Bosham, Emsworth, Dell Quay – never the same place twice. Selwyn was shown the six foot square secret hideaway in Bosham, into which he climbed but does not give a hint as to its whereabouts! The contraband was then moved, probably by night, to another secret hideaway near Rogate for later transfer to London.

There have been many rumours of the smugglers using underground passages which were alleged to run from the church to The Anchor and northwards up to the main road. When James Duke was doing some trenching in the garden of Quay Cottage behind the ancient wall on the High Street opposite the church, the ground suddenly caved in and he fell into a hole. Duke found himself in a large cellar which was thought to be a left over from the monks' cells which had been in that area. Rescued unhurt, the hole was filled in. Selwyn himself recalls hearing of people falling into other tunnels and only as recently as the 1980s there was a report of workmen laying sewage pipes in the garden of a house near the old Congregational Church, coming upon an underground tunnel running north/south. Rosie Frogbrook had in her possession a piece of stalactite which her mother, as a child, had broken off one of the walls of a tunnel which ran between the church and The Anchor.

The local constabulary, not surprisingly, was always on the lookout for such contraband and it took Lloyd a long time to realise why the local populace was so interested and knowledgeable on the whereabouts of the local Bobbie (policeman) or Customs Officers! Until comparatively recently, Bosham had always had its own policeman – the Police House was in Brooks Lane but this has now been sold.

During the 2nd World War John Yates recalls, as a school boy, Mr. Scales, the school master, organising his pupils to work two days a week in the grounds of Mr. Brinkmans nurseries on the Main Road, growing vegetables – 'digging for Victory' as it was known.

In the holidays, when there was the threat of invasion, under the direction of Mr. Scales, Yates helped build a gun post in Gover's field behind Green Lane. Also the boys had to fill sandbags which were placed all over the Broadbridge Farm fields to prevent enemy gliders landing. In 1940, every signpost in the country was also removed to confuse any enemy parachutists who might drop from the skies. There was a searchlight battery behind Brooks Farm, north of the main road, which received two hits by blast bombs. The two carthorses belonging to Touzer Wilkins were the only casualties. Unable to read or write, Touzer could plough a straight furrow better than anyone and the loss of these horses caused him terrible distress. The houses that were damaged by these bombs became the site of St. Nicholas Church Hall. The local children enjoyed a bit of souvenir hunting when a German dive bomber crash landed in September, 1940, just north of the railway crossing at Bosham Station. The crew of four climbed out and were taken into custody by the police. A group of Bosham lads were blackberrying in the area at the time and it was not long before they were running over the electrified line to collect a sizeable quantity of souvenirs from the German aircraft. A few months before this incident, another German Junkers 88 aircraft was shot down and landed in Mudberry Farm.

Charles Stenning recalls coming to Bosham in 1940 as a lorry driver, working fourteen to sixteen hours a day with only one half day off a week. The village bustled with activity with troops billeted everywhere – in empty houses and camping in the fields. The old vicarage, now Walton House, was requisitioned for the army. There was a Bosham Home Guard – B Company 1st (Chichester Battery) with three colonels (no doubt retired) with Captain Mussared as 2nd in command. Platoon commanders included Lt. C.W. Scales, the school master and George Redman, the blacksmith. Their H.Q. was Broadbridge Farm and there were a total of a hundred and fifty five men. One

wonders with what they were armed! Formed in May 1940 when there was a very real threat of invasion by the Germans, they were stood down in December 1944.

During those war years, it was mandatory for everyone to carry identity cards and gas masks with them wherever they went. Food was rationed, but in the rural communities people had a few chickens in their back gardens and thus had extra eggs in the laying season. Eggs could be preserved in buckets of isinglass, a preservative. These eggs were no good for boiling or frying but

One of the local characters in a mural painted by Rex Whistler on the wall of the Ship in June 1944

could be used for scrambling or cake making. People would club together and buy a pig, feed it on the kitchen leftovers, then share the meat of the animal between themselves when the pig was killed. Parts of the pig not immediately eaten could be preserved in baths of saltpetre. Deep freezes had not arrived yet!

Villagers recall the frequent air raids over Portsmouth and seeing the sky bright red from the burning buildings. The Ship Inn in the High Street became the Old Ship Club, an officers' club run by Trevor and Nancy Moorhouse. Officers from Tangmere and Thorney Island came here for a few hours of rest and relaxation, play games and chat. Rex Whistler, the well known artist, visited the club a few times while awaiting embarkation to France after the D-Day landings on June 4th 1944. During those ten days, before being killed in action, he painted a mural on the wall depicting some of the local characters. Before the Ship Club closed down in 1959, by which time it had become a social club, it had many distinguished members including the Marquis of Milford Haven, Lord Portal and General Sir Brian Horrocks. Princess Margaret, sister of Queen Elizabeth, was a dining guest at the club on one occasion.

The men of Bosham's Home Guard in 1940

The Land Army girls, who lived in the Red House immediately opposite the Anchor on the other side of the creek, usually went to the Anchor for their entertainment and refreshment.

D-Day was celebrated by an enormous bonfire in the High Street when the Moorhouses of The Ship Club threw in the club's blackout curtains and Jean Ogilvie who lived a few days away in The Castle in the High Street remembers, in all the excitement, throwing her school trunk into the blaze. In the midst of the hilarity, a car suddenly appeared, drove at top speed down to the Quay, a stranger climbed out of the car and dived into the mud – he was hauled out, unhurt but covered in black slime. Such was the excitement of the day.

Don Pratt recalls a village party held a few days after VE Day in the gardens of the former vicarage, now Walton House, which the Canadian army had just vacated. A barrel organ was borrowed and pushed around the village, accompanied by children holding the edges of a large sheet into which everyone was asked to throw a few pennies to buy the necessary for such a party. Mothers and housewives who had a few ounces of sugar, butter or any foodstuff to spare from their food rations, gave or baked cakes, biscuits and sandwiches to which the whole village came for this great celebration – after six years of war it needed a good party to cheer everyone up.

After the 2nd World War, things changed considerably. The populace became even more mobile as more and more people acquired cars. People no longed worked within a mile or two of their homes, but in towns ten and twenty miles away where industries and business' were started and this enabled people to continue to live in Bosham. The former fishermen's cottages which previously had fetched, when sold, only a few hundred pounds became the much sought after weekend cottages costing thousands of pounds for the yachtsmen who worked in London or other large cities. Invariably these people contributed little to the local economy for the weekenders arrived with their food and friends on Friday evening, to depart on Sunday evening having probably bought little else but a daily paper and some milk during their forty eight

Programme of Events during the

SILVER JUBILEE CELEBRATIONS

in

BOSHAM

Friday 3rd to Tuesday 7th June 1977

Price 10 pence

+

We offer Her Majesty greetings and congratulations on the occasion of her Silver Jubilee from her loyal subjects in Bosham.

hours in the village. Perhaps in some ways these yachtsmen did save the village from the snack bars and cafes, from the juke boxes and the sun seekers. The lack of a sandy beach has, on the whole, drawn only those who come to mess about in boats, enjoy the Bosham scene and partake of refreshment from one of the four remaining hostelries. The many owner-managed local grocery shops closed down one by one, as the locals in their cars sought the attractions of cheap supermarkets where there was a greater selection of goods.

However, even these changes did not stop some people in Bosham celebrating Queen Elizabeth II's Coronation in 1953 when the mothers of those children who lived in Critchfield Road only organised a party in Chapel Hall, Bosham Lane, when each child was given a celebratory mug.

Twenty five years later, for the Queen's Silver Jubilee, under the direction of Commander Richard Rycroft, a splendid day of celebration was almost ruined by gale force winds and driving rain. There was a Flower Festival in the church, a mother and toddler's picnic was held on Quay Meadow while the kite flying competitions proved very hectic in the strong winds.

Bosham was also halved in size as the villages of Chidham and Fishbourne formed their own parish councils independent of Bosham, although the people from these areas, unless they went into Chichester, still came to Bosham for some of their minor shopping requirements.

The village now has a mini-market and a farm shop each open from early morning to late at night, seven

A party given for the Coronation of Queen Elizabeth II in 1953 in the Congregational Hall, Bosham Lane

days a week. In the 1970s a craft centre, Bosham Walk, was built from old bricks and timbers, which now draws thousands of visitors. There are a number of places where light meals and teas can be bought, while the three pubs and the more exclusive Millstream Hotel do a roaring trade, particularly in the summer.

Entertainment is no longer a village enterprise – the television had opened the wider world to the people of Bosham – many emigrated to the far away continents of Australia and North America, particularly after the 2nd World War. A holiday was no longer a day return on the railway to Brighton or Portsmouth but, after a few hours in an aeroplane, a week in Spain or Greece. Large housing estates were built on the fields north of the now Millstream Hotel at Moreton Road, on Fairfield Road, the field on which the annual fairs had been held, as well as in the area where Broadbridge Mill once stood, to cope with the expanding population. The old families had moved away from the houses along the shore, the High Street and Bosham Lane to disperse to other parts of the village or elsewhere for their former homes to be occupied by the weekenders and the retired.

Organizations and societies grew in number. There were the Cricket and Football Clubs, the Women's Institute, a Horticultural Society, a Youth Club, The Guides and Brownies, a flower Club and more recently keep fit classes, badminton and bowls. The new village hall, built in 1996, has become the centre for many more village activities and is also popular for wedding receptions. The Monday Club for the over 60s meets in St. Nicholas Church Hall at Broadbridge every Monday throughout the year. There is still the annual regatta organised by the Bosham Sailing Club, while hundreds attend the annual bonfire nights also organised by this Club when silver collections are made for various local charities. The church fêtes, held in the Manor House garden continue, raising not just hundreds but thosands of pounds for the benefit of the church. More about these activities can be found in Chapter 14.

Bosham had two Royal visits in the 20th century. August 1923 saw Queen Mary, Consort of King George Vth, pay a fleeting visit to Bosham. She was escorted round the village by Henry Henshall, the artist whose sketches featured in the Rev.

Mr & Mrs Gregory Major, who entertained Queen Elizabeth to tea in their home Bychurch, in December 1939

MacDermott's book on Bosham Church. Sixteen years later in December 1939 Queen Elizabeth, Consort of King George VIth, visited Bosham. As well as walking round the village she had a cup of tea in the home of Mr. &and Mrs. Gregory Major at Bychurch (now called Galleon House) in the High Street.(See Chapter 5 - Church Visitors).

Communications have also speeded up – no longer does it take six weeks for a letter to reach Australia as it did at the turn of the century, nor a week for an air mail letter in the 1950s. By the year 2000, for just one pound or so a telephone call could be made to the Antipodes or for a few pence one was able to send and receive a reply by electronic mail (e-mail) to

Queen Elizabeth, consort of King George VI, at the home of Mr & Mrs Gregory Major at Bychurch, now part of Galleon House, in December 1939.
Picture by Courtesy of the Chichester Observer

anywhere in the world within a few seconds. The advent of computers also enabled a large number of people to work from home. So life is turning full circle with families returning to the villages and the need for weekending is receding.

On Saturday 22nd July 2000, a warm and sunny day, Bosham celebrated the millennium in great style with floats representing many incidents from Bosham's history paraded through the streets. Races and competitions were held on Quay Meadow, and on the water dozens of boats were dressed overall. In the church the millennium map made by the W.I. Art Group was displayed together with photographs of the village taken during the previous hundred years.

Otherwise the beginning of the 21st century saw Bosham, still a comparatively quiet place, with many visitors strolling around the shore enjoying the serenity of the old church, the hustle and bustle of dozens of sailing dinghies hoisting their sails on the Quay or the peace of the High Street. Hopefully visitors do not park their cars below the high water mark to be swamped at times of high tide – a regular occurrence in spite of the notices. Until the 1970s, there was not even a permanent café where one could get a cup of tea, but now there are a number of places dispensing the time honoured English tradition of a cup of tea.

CHAPTER 8

Shopping
over the centuries

Positioned as it is on the south coast of England, nestled in the safe environment of Chichester Harbour with a good deep water anchorage, Bosham has been an excellent point for trade between the continent of Europe and the English mainland for many centuries. Two and three thousand years ago, itinerant travellers trading in metal and pottery landed in Bosham to carry their goods inland to barter with the locals. Although there is evidence of cooking pots being imported into England in Saxon times, pots were made locally using Chichester Harbour clay with local limestone and then exported to the continent. As has been stated elsewhere in this book, due to the excellent soil and the long sun hours along the coastal plain, the corn from this area proved a popular export, at one time feeding some of the Roman armies of north-west Europe. In the 8th century Bosham was the sixth most important town in Sussex.

Foodstuffs were taken into the Chichester market which was held every Wednesday. At the time of Henry VIII (reigned 1509-47) beef, pork and lamb were only a halfpenny for a pound weight. Recently a number of sewing needles were found in the brook by the Mill House - sewing needles were made in Chichester until the time of the Civil War; this suggests that there were local seamstresses.

As life became more sophisticated, the housewives who had started a business by selling food surplus to their own requirements from their back door or bartering with the neighbours, moved their trading activities into the front room, which then became a local shop. Anyone with any sort of garden would have grown more than enough vegetables for their own use for the whole year, preserving and storing sufficient for the winter months, any surplus being sold off.

The village itself would have been self-sufficient for everyone's daily needs, with corn grown and milled locally and, for those who did not bake their own, bakeries were established to do just that. With fishing one of the main occupations, while the fishermens' shore-side cottages had no gardens, so fish could have been bartered for vegetables, chickens and eggs for oysters and mackerel for flour, as examples.

In the early 20th century, Trixie Balchin remembers the fishermen's wives walking around the village with pannier baskets on their heads, filled with the fish of the day. Both Trixie and Rosie Frogbrook also remember being sent around to Mrs. Hoskins who lived in what had been the Poor Houses, off the High Street, now known as Harbour Cottages, to get 2/- (20p) worth of fish, usually a basketful of bass or plaice. Ellen Sheen also recalls buying fish direct from the fishermen as soon as the catch was landed. On Chichester's market day, Mrs. Hoskins with her flat topped wooden cart laden with fish, trundled it up to the station, put cart, fish and herself on the train and sold the fish in the market there. Prior to the days of the arrival of the train services, foodstuffs would have been taken on foot into Chichester.

For those items not available locally like dress materials and knitting yarns, travelling salesmen, walking from village to village, would bring these commodities as well as saucepans, crockery and cutlery, to sell to the locals. Furniture was made locally by the village carpenter although a lot of it would have been passed down through the families. Slowly, local shops opened and by the mid 1850s there were a number of them in the village. In the census return of 1851 as well as in Kellys' directories of that time, there are listed dressmakers, milliners, tailors and shoemakers as well as no less than four bakers and three grocers. Alfred Hickman was the village bootmaker, while his son was the boatyard blacksmith at the Apps Shipyard on Quay Meadow. Four generations of the Redman family

The Swan Inn on the (far) right, with the station in the background. In between was the railway goods yard. The notice on the left of picture, advertises a railway excursion

operated a forge in Walton Lane as well as in Fishbourne, a few houses west of the Globe Inn, which until recently was part of the Parish of Bosham. As well as shoeing the farm horses, the forge would have done all the local metal repair work. The forge in Walton Lane was pulled down in the early 1970s, while the Fishbourne one is now a private house.

Prior to 1846, when the first train service operated through the village, the mail for the village came by the coaches which ran from Brighton to Portsmouth along the turnpike road (previously the A27, now A259). The use of the mail coaches ceased with the arrival of the train service – the first one was run by the London Brighton and South Coast Railway coming through Bosham in March, 1847, on the Chichester/Portsmouth line. This is no doubt the reason for the Mail Office at the time being in the Swan Inn for it was one of the coaching inns of the 18th century. In the Post Office Directory of 1852, the Bosham entry lists William Collins of the White Swan as the postmaster for the letter, money order and telegraph offices. There was also a telegraph office at the station for inter-station communication but later the railway company permitted its use for private telegrams. In 1874, the post office moved to the Railway Station at Broadbridge, with Frank Kinch as the sub-postmaster. Between 1891 and 1895, a new post office was opened in Bosham Lane, a few doors from the Congregational church, in a grocer's shop owned by a widow, Sophia Collins.

The shop bore many names over the decades - Collins' Stores, Country Stores, Bosham Stores and Coward's Stores. It is now a private house called Berkeley Cottage. Harry Collins, Sophia's son, became the first sub-postmaster in his mother's store. The post office continued here under his son, also Harry, until his death in 1946. It was also here that the first telephone exchange was installed in the front room of the house. Later a telephone box was placed outside the shop. In 1947 this post office was transferred to the High Street, where it remained until about 1995 when it too closed.

Polly (Pauline) Collins, daughter of the Postmaster of Bosham, outside her father's shop in Bosham Lane. She delivered the post and telegrams for her father.

In 1924 Bosham Station Post Office was taken over by Leonard Carpenter who ran a confectioner's shop in one of the three shops in Station Road, just a few yards from the railway station. The sub-postmaster of this office changed with the ownership of the shop. In 1963, Mr. Forbes sold the newsagents shop but not before he had built an addition to the north side of his shop to where he transferred the post office and remained the sub-postmaster. In April 1992 Mr. Forbes retired and this post office was moved to the Bosham Farm Shop in Delling Lane.

In the 1890s there was no butcher in Bosham, so on Friday mornings, Mr. Goodger of West Ashling used to set up a butcher's shop in the oyster sorting barn on Shore Road, where now there is a house called Oysters. The Hon. C.P.F. Berkeley of Old Park, was a regular customer of Mr. Goodger. In an account dated 31st December, 1895, Mr. Berkeley bought £5 worth of meat from this butcher. There was an alternative to Mr. Goodger's meat for Mr. J.R. Mant, butcher of Emsworth, advertised prime Devon beef while Charlie Howard of 81 North Street, Chichester, advertised fine Southdown mutton – 'only the finest Home-grown Meat supplied' so the advertisement read.

Mr. Ayling of Eastgate, Chichester, wholesale and retail poulterer in 1896 sold, to the owner of Old Park, 56 pheasants at 2/3d each (11p.) and 14 hares at 3/- (33p.) each. Did they have a banquet at Old Park about that time? Mr. Berkeley patronised other local grocers: in the account book of 1891, Mr. Berkeley bought from Mr. C.J. Fondell milk at 2d. a pint, cream at 3d., butter at 2/- (10p) a pound weight. The household consumed two to three pints of milk a day

Mr. Berkeley also made payments to Sadlers, the corn merchants in Chichester for the following seeds and seedlings: '7 pounds swedes, 2 ounces

The Carpenter family in a field at Broadbridge. The little child is their daughter, Joyce, who was to become Mrs Stant and a one time chairman of the West Sussex Federation of Womens' Institutes

1.Bosham Lane some time in the 1920s. Collins Stores is on the left with the village's first telephone box.On the right is the dairy run by the Collins family. After the 2nd World War it was leased out as a tearoom.

Next door is the garage which housed the fire engine bought by Gerald Marcuse in 1947. (See page 144)

2. The window of the Country Stores (formerly H.Collins Stores)

3. The shops in Station Road in 1991. They include a sweet shop, a newsagents and the Co-op.

Drumhead cabbage and 1000 heads of cabbage', while Martin Coombes was paid five shillings (25p) for three days work.

In the Old Park accounts, still retained in the Muniment Room of Berkeley Castle in Gloucestershire, there were a number of references to the accounts of Mr. Merrett who was paid £1.16.0 (£1.80p) for grinding corn, while Mr. Baker, the chemist, was paid £1.1.6 (£1.7.5p) – one wonders what potions the household purchased from him? There was also a chemist shop in Delling Lane, one of the three shops south of The Swan. Mr. Scutt, coal merchant who had his depot where now the Bosham Service Station is in Bosham Lane, was paid £3.3.4 (£1.16p) for about two tons of coal. A lot of these items were entered in a small threepenny cash book and contained payments for washing 13s.6d, (67.5 p) four weeks of house cleaning £1, watercress 3d. (1p) and a telegram 1/- (5p).

Richardson's, which had been on the High Path, the building that juts out over the raised walkway along Shore Road, sold their shop there and, as a result of inheriting some money, built a new shop in Bosham Lane and had a trade brochure printed. These brochures were probably given to their regular clients at Christmas time and included photographs of Bosham taken before 1901. In Jan 1893 Mr. Berkeley bought £7.7s0d (£7.35p) of goods from H. Richardson, Grocer, Provision Dealer, Draper and Boot Factor. Richardson also advertised 'New Zealand mutton in prime condition' legs at 6d(2.5p.) a pound weight, shoulders 5d a pound (2p.) and necks at 4d a pound (nearly 2p.). He then named his shop the General Supply Stores and later sold the business to Mr. Broadbridge who renamed it Broadbridge Stores.

The two Cowards sisters took over Harry Collins' shop near the Congregational Church in Bosham after the 2nd World War. They also ran the Bosham Dairy opposite and had a twice daily milk delivery around the village. The dairy was later to become for many years the only tea room in Bosham – but the times at which it was open were variable, dependent on the whims of the proprietor; at the time the only place in the village where one could get a cup of tea! As a child, Gertrude Arnell, born in 1888, recalls buying one penny's worth of milk from the back door of the Mill House while Mrs Hector (née Woods), born in the early 1900s, recalls collecting butter from the same place; milk was also delivered direct to her childhood home, Primrose Cottage on the High Path or Trippet, as it is now known.

For many years Annie Stoveld ran a grocer's shop in the High Street, which was also the village sweet shop. The house now called Galleon House, still has the same shop window, on which there is a preservation order. Behind were the shelves on which were displayed the large glass bottles filled with wrapped sweets, such as barley sugar, pear and fruit-drops, sold to the youngsters at the price of so many sweets for a farthing (one quarter of an old penny). If your weekly pocket money was only one penny per week, it was more satisfying to spend your precious money in quarters. There was also a grocer's shop over on Gosportside on the south side of Shore Road, which served the needs of those who lived on that side of the creek.

There was Sadler's in Station Road, now the Co-op , as well as Smallbones, newsagents, afterwards run by the Sweets, which the Luscombes now own.

There was, for a short time, a small branch of the then well-known chain of shops, the International Stores, at the corner of North Road and the former main road, now Penwarden Way, in what had been More's Stores.

In the Regatta Programme for 1908, Henry Follett, Grocer and Provision Merchant of the High Street Bosham advertised 'Long's Ales and Stouts'. It is

Henry Follet with his daughter Elsie in front of his shop - Follet's Stores in the High Street. Pictured between 1902 & 1911.

LONG'S
Ales and Stouts.

Approved and Recommended by the British Analytical Control . . . . .

Local Agent—HENRY FOLLETT,
Grocer and Provision Merchant,
HIGH STREET, BOSHAM.

Galleon House, the former grocery shop and sweet shop in the High Street

on record that in the 15th century beers and wines were imported from the continent in ships largely Guernsey registered. In July 1393 the cost of twelve barrels of imported beer was 20s (£1). Beer was usually brewed by each individual inn, though once the Henty Brewery opened up in Westgate, Chichester, this was sold in some of the Bosham pubs. Other advertisements in the Regatta programme were for Bongola Tea at 1s.6d (7.5p) a pound weight, A.G. Coombes for Ladies Costumes from fifty shillings (£2.50) while Ern. Miles, Hatter and Hosier, of 17 South Street, Chichester, advertised smart suitings, golfing hosiery and rainproof coats. There was for many years a small drapers' shop in Station Road, a few yards from the railway station, run by Ada Grovett. She sold wool and knitting patterns, dress materials and underwear together with all manner of needles and cottons - this is now a fish and chip shop.

In the 1950s there were six grocers' shops in the village – Folletts, rebuilt in 1947 to become Hines Stores in the High Street, Broadbridges at the bottom of Bosham Lane, Coward's and two in Station Road. Mrs. Harding built a small wooden hut as a grocer's shop in Delling Lane south of the Swan Inn. In due course, the Hardings built a bigger shop next door, while Vic, their son, ran a barber's shop in the hut. Later the latter was to become a shoe shop run by Mr. Blakemore where he repaired shoes or did any other leather work required. This hut was pulled down and the ground floor of the new building is now

an Indian takeaway, while Harding's, now much enlarged, is a furniture shop. Veale's, the butchers, was the third shop of the group, which was taken over by Mr. and Mrs. Hatt. Mrs. Hatt did a twice weekly delivery round the village – the ordered meat was put on a piece of greaseproof paper, the price written on a little chit which was fixed to the meat with a pin - the customer provided a plate for the meat when it was delivered. This form of delivering meat would give today's food and hygiene inspectors apoplexy!

In the 1930s, two Austrian gentlemen ran a cheese factory making "Chissick Cheese" in Broadbridge Farmhouse next door to the present Bosham Farm Shop. The cheese was not very popular. Then two to three days before the declaration of war in 1939, the men disappeared and the local gossip was that they had been spies. The small factory continued to make cheese for some time after the war until the factory, together with Broadbridge House next door, was demolished.

There were a number of bakers in Bosham - in 1861 Ernest Purver ran a bakery in Rose Cottage, Bosham Lane. (There were three Rose Cottages then - one next door to The Berkeley Arms and another behind the house St. Martins on the High Street).After the death in 1888 of George Purver, his widow, Sarah, endeavored to carry on the business with the help of her son-in-law, Ernest Layzell, who gave up his job as a clerk with the railway company to help her. However, he was no baker, and got into severe trouble with the authorities for adding mashed potato to the dough in order to make the bread look whiter. The bakery was sold, he returned to his job with the railway company and his wife Alice became one of the teachers at the National School at the top of the creek, where Eva Layzell, later Eva Purser, was a pupil. By 1899 Weeks was the baker in this house followed by a succession of other owners. In 1901 it had become Sparks, followed by Arthur Beardwell, who sold it to the Chichester bakery, Spurriers. In 1915 Colebournes ran the business as Ye Olde Bosham Tea Shoppe with tables in the garden where they served tea on warm summer days. Colebourne replaced his horse and cart with a Ford van for the daily deliveries of bread and cakes - no doubt one of the first motor delivery vans to operate in Bosham. The ground flour for this bakery came from Mr. Gatehouse at Broadbridge Mill.

Also the Fishbourne bakery called Coopers delivered daily to Bosham with horse and cart. At the turn of the 20th century, a four pound (weight) loaf of bread cost fourpence three farthings (5p) and hot cross buns one penny each 'made from pure lard' so the advertisement read. In the Kelly's Directory there is a bakery listed at the house afterwards called The Poplars recently re-named The Old Bakehouse, in Bosham Lane, run by Mr. Merston. In 1919 Vokes of Chichester had a daily bread delivery round in the village by horse and cart - if you bought a bag of flour from them, you got a coupon - if by Christmas you had collected enough coupons you were given a cake.

After the end of the 2nd World War, most of the shops in

Arthur Colebourne stands with Len Carpenter beside his new Ford van. The old handcart stands in the background. The small boy standing on the wall is Leslie, Arthur Colebourne's second son.

Chichester, particularly the food shops, were delivering to the village once or twice a week. There were branches of two banks in Bosham which opened for a few hours a week. Lloyds Bank was in the High Street, later moving to a room in Glenco next door to Broadbridge Stores in Bosham Lane where Barclays Bank already had a room. Both branches were closed in the 1960s. As the population became more mobile and supermarkets opened in Chichester, one by one the old grocers shops closed as they could not compete on price. The Post Office/newsagents in the High Street took to stocking very basic food stuffs for a short time but that too closed in about 1995 and Bosham was left with just the one post office in Station Road

Chichester Dairies, whose Tubercular Tested milk came from Broadbridge Farm, marketed all the locally produced milk in their depot in Chichester and with the Co-op, each had a daily milk delivery covering the whole village – the milk vans also carried such items as bread, butter and soft drinks. Now there is just the one company – the Co-op doing a much reduced daily round – for milk is now cheaper in the supermarkets. The Co-op remains in business in Station Road, as well as the newsagents, Luscombes, who also sell sweets and wine and is open seven days a week from early morning to late at night.

A farm shop was opened up in what had been the Broadbridge Farm barns in Delling Lane in the mid- 1970s. This shop has now become a mini food market selling a very wide variety of goods, which, in including the Bosham Station Post Office, has made this enterprise the major shop in the village.

Frank Sylvester doing his daily milk round with his pony and trap

Above: The High Street in about 1955. A branch of Lloyds Bank is on the left of the picture

Bosham Lane at the times of high spring tides. On the right is Pedlar's Garage with a petrol pump. It is here that Bosham Walk has been built

The Farm Shop also sells newspapers, hires out videos, has a licence for selling wines and spirits and is open fourteen hours a day seven days a week.

In 1978, an arts and craft centre was built on the site of the former petrol pump and fire station at the end of Bosham Lane. In constructing the building, old bricks and timbers were utilised as far as was possible, resulting in a building that looks much older than it is. Here all manner of craft items are sold which include small antiques, a book stall, artists paraphernalia, herbs remedies, jewellery and cosmetics, as well as a dress shop and a tea-room.

Thus at the turn of the 21st century, Bosham has as few shops as there were in the village in 1800 though a more mobile population has increased fourfold in the last two hundred years.

A fisherman scrubbing his boat on the shore beside Quay Cottage

CHAPTER 9
Some work of Noble Note Tennyson

Over the centuries, the three principal occupations of the people of Bosham were fishing, boat-building and farming. These continued as the main forms of employment until well after the 2nd World War. Now at the beginning of the 21st century, the only one still active is farming, although instead of numerous tenant farmers under no more than two landlords, the Berkeleys' and later the Cheesmans, there is now only one resident farmer working his own or rented land. In the 1899 Kelly's directory, there were ten farmers, seven master mariners and two ship-builders listed, though there are known to have been more of the latter.

Fishing must have gone on since time immemorial, but the fish were sold only locally or in the Chichester market until the arrival of the trains in 1847. It was then possible to get

Ned Coombes nicknamed 'Sugar Plum'. He owned one of the largest oyster boats in the harbour - some 30 feet (just over nine metres) long

the fish, including oysters, to London in one day; this resulted in a great expansion of the trade. Today there are few fishing boats to be seen in the harbour and they are largely for pleasure rather than profit.

There was a large ship-building industry with four or five yards building everything from small dinghies to large fishing boats and trading schooners, all constructed in wood. After the 2nd World War, the industry turned to building pleasure yachts, initially in wood but latterly in fibreglass, but this activity too has ceased and there are now no working shipyards on the Bosham shores. In the 16th and 17th centuries there were blacksmiths, wheel-wrights, maltsters, fishermen and mariners, details of which were obtained from wills and inventories, but no mention of ship-builders.

Almost all the fishermen in Bosham were 'Men of Bosham' - there are few holders of this title today. The origin of the rights of The Men is lost in the mists of time; it certainly existed before 1066 as they were first mentioned by King Caedwalla of Wessex (685-88). The charter by which these Men hold their rights was re-enacted three times - by Henry II (1153-89), Queen Elizabeth I in 1568 and by James I in 1607. The Men, in order to qualify, must have been born in Bosham, be the son of a Man of Bosham and earn their living as seafarers, i.e. as a seamen, by fishing, and/or boat building. The Charter states that 'all 'Men and Tenants of the Ancient Demesne (demesnes were manors owned by the Crown during the reigns of Edward the Confessor and William I) of the aforesaid Crown have been accustomed... to be exempt from...' and lists all manner of privileges. For example, they were exempt from paying for their Member of Parliament, (the first parliament sat in the 13th century) nor required to do jury service. (Jury service was thought to have been brought in by William the Conqueror; anyhow by the Jury Act of 1892, all such rights held by individuals were repealed.) In addition The Men were allowed throughout England free toll, tollage, panage, (payment usually made by tenants to the lord for the right to graze pigs in the lord's woods), murage (a tax paid for maintaining town and city walls) and were allowed to fish and to moor their boats without payment of any taxes throughout the realm. Today the only privileges The Men hold are free anchorage or payment of any tax for fishing and wildfowling within Chichester Harbour. For years, the Chichester Corporation had managed the harbour in a fairly loose manner ever since James II had decreed that all ships coming into Chichester Harbour must go through customs at the Port of Dell Quay, thus giving the Chichester Corporation the right to collect any taxes so generated. (It is thought that there were Customs sub-stations around the harbour, possibly one on Bosham Hoe.) In 1938, the Corporation sought to legitimise these rights by Act of Parliament known as the Chichester Corporation Bill. This Act would have effectively removed the few remaining rights that the Men of Bosham still held. To this end, fifty Men of Bosham petitioned the House of Lords against this Bill. Each petitioner contributed three shillings and threepence (16p) towards the legal costs while a large majority of them could sign only with a cross as they were unable to write their own names. The matter was settled out of court in a 'Without Prejudice' letter dated 4th May, 1938. This letter agreed that in no way would the Chichester Corporation interfere with the rights of the Men of Bosham within Chichester Harbour unless the Men took any action which would hinder safe navigation in these waters. The only tax for which they would be required to pay would be when they operated their boats for pleasure or were plied for hire.

The seaman, in order to obtain his certificate as a Man of Bosham, had to

COPY OF THE

Charter of Bosham.

JAMES, by the Grace of God, of England, Scotland, France, and Ireland, King,
Defender of the Faith, &c.

"To All and singular Sheriffs, Mayors, Bailiefs, Constables, Officers and all other loving Subjects, as well within or without our liberties to whom these Presents shall come, Greeting. Whereas according to the Custom of our Realm of England hitherto held and obtained all men and Tenants of the Antient Demesme of the Crown of England have been and ought to be free of Toll, Tollage, Pannage, Murage, Carriage and passage thro' our Realm of England and also according to the aforesaid custom all Men and Tenants of the antient Demesne of the aforesaid Crown have been accustomed from the time whereof the Memory of Man is not to the contrary to be exempt from contributing to the Expences of our Parliament or our Progenitors formerly Kings of England or assembling with the Commons of the said Kingdom; and also according to the said Custom the Men and Tenants of the Manors which are the antient Demesne of our aforesaid Crown, for their Lands and Tenaments which are held of the same Manors ought not to be put in Assizes, Juries, or Recognizances unless in those of their own Manor or Court. And as well for that the Manor of BOSHAM with its Appertenances in the County of Sussex, is of the antient Demesne of our Crown existing as for the Easements Granted by our beloved Sister the LADY ELIZABETH late Queen of England in her Chancery by the Treasurer of the Exchequer Chamber as of her Command then sent."

"We Will enjoin and command Ye that all and singular Men and Tenants of the Manor of Bosham aforesaid be permitted to be exempt from Homage or Payment of tolls, Tollage, Pannage, Murage or other thing for Carriage, Passage of Goods, or any other thing throughout our aforesaid Realm. And also from the expences of Soldiers. And also that the same Men and Tenants of the said Manor shall be exempt from Assizes, Juries and Recognizances without the Court held for the same Manor (unless in it, in which in the said Manor, will or ought to be held one) contrary to the above said Custom unless the Lands or Tenaments held of any other Tenure for which according to the form of the Statute of the Common Council of our Realm of England is provided in Juries, or Recognizances ought there to be put.—And if the aforesaid Men and Tenants of the Manor of Bosham aforesaid shall upon those occasions or any other be Charged, Rated or Impannelled, that YE do ease them without delay."

In Witness whereof we have caused these our Letters to be made Patent. Witness ourself at Westminster the 10th, day of January in the Fourth Year of our Reign over England, France, Ireland &c. &c. &c.

(Signed) CLAPHAM.

Grandpa Major repairing his nets

again by Act of Parliament, the Chichester Harbour Conservancy was created, the vetting of qualifications was taken over by the Harbour Conservancy. Recently, a successful application was made to be a Man of Bosham by Mark Murray Brown through his mother, the daughter of Edward Gilby, a Man of Bosham. Although documents state that applications for this right should be through the lineal line, it had always been through the direct male line. However, in this age of equality of the sexes, it would be difficult for this request to be refused but may well open the way for applications by seafaring daughters of Men of Bosham to apply for the title. Mark Murray Brown manages the Cobnor Activities Centre and is now able to have a mooring in the harbour without payment of any harbour dues.

satisfy two Justices of the Peace acting for the western division of the County of West Sussex, that he was born in Bosham, the son of a Man of Bosham and that he had, prior to 1937, earned his livelihood in fishing, yachting or boating in the harbour. When in 1971,

Oyster fishing was another successful industry. In mediaeval times, oysters were an important part of the diet of the locals. At the turn of the 20th century, Bosham was second only to Whitstable in the oyster trade operated by about forty boats. Sometime after 1870 a Bosham Dredgermen's Co-operative was formed and the A shares, known as profit shares, were distributed for nominal sums, while the B shares, known as working shares with a

The Oyster Barn, one of the buildings where oysters were sorted

1. Bill and Jack Arnold loading nets before going out oyster dredging

2. Repairing fishing nets

3. B (Working) Share Certificate of William Coombes

4. Arthur White and Charlie Stoveld start shrimping

101

nominal value £5, were only for those actively engaged in the industry. There were strict rules governing the operations and regular inspections were made of the oysters. The trade only operated in the winter, while during the summer months, the oyster fishermen crewed in the large yachts which sailed and raced in the Solent earning £1.5s.0 (£1.25p.) a week, while as oystermen they earned 5s (25p) for every four hundred oysters landed. The names of the yachts in which they crewed are remembered in the new roads around Fairfield Road.

The young oysters were brought over from the French coast and placed in nursery beds off Rookwood in the south-eastern part of the harbour, where a regular guard, known as the watch boat, was kept on the oyster beds. After three years the oysters were again dredged up and placed in beds up School Rithe and Cut Mill Creek, where they were left for three weeks to clean themselves. According to requirements, the oysters were dredged up and sorted in one of the oysters barns, one of which

Packing oysters on the quay

is the Raptackle on the Quay, or in a barn where now a house called 'Oysters' on Shore Road has been built. Those orders that were to go further afield by train were put in pannier baskets, placed on the backs of donkeys and taken to the railway station. There is evidence that in the 18th century, oysters were exported to Holland and the Low Countries. Unfortunately after limpets attacked the molluscs, the industry came to an end in 1921. The oyster trade is returning to Chichester Harbour, but as far as is known, there are no Bosham boats involved.

Dublin Bay prawns were another shellfish found locally, but not to a very large extent. Eva Purser recalls that as a child these larger prawns were given to them for tea so often that she found herself hating them. There were also a number of local boats employed in other forms of fishing which went further afield into the Solent and English Channel. They were normally away for four or five days a week, loaded with sufficient food prepared by their wives, to last them until their return. They landed these catches daily in either Southampton or Portsmouth. Mrs. Ellen Sheen recalled going down to Bosham Quay when the fishing boats came in and buying plaice, dabs, flounders, bass, eel and shrimps - a glassful of the latter cost one penny. In one of the many old documents on fishing, it is recorded that the Lord of the Manor and the vicar were each entitled to one tenth of every catch.

Boat building also gave many local men employment. Building

boats must have gone on here ever since man arrived in the area and chiselled out with flints the centre of a tree trunk to form a canoe-type boat. We know that Harold kept his fleet in Bosham and some if not all of his ships were likely to have been built here. Two 100-ton ships are thought to have been built in Bosham for the Navy and, manned by local men, sailed against the Spanish in the Armada in 1588.

One of the earliest yards in Bosham must have been what became the Apps Shipyard which is on the north side of Quay Meadow and which was run for many years by Thomas Apps - the slipway and a capstan used in the yard are still to be seen within the grounds of the house, The Slip, which was built on the site. The yard workshop is now a private house called The Barn. The blacksmith's forge, immediately behind the War Memorial on Quay Meadow, is now used as a garden shed by the Iveagh family whose company, The Manor of Bosham Ltd., own the property, so a company is effectively the Lord of the Manor. The Apps shipyard in Bosham may have started as far back as the late 1700s, for William and Sarah Apps settled in Bosham and their second child, a son also called William, was born here in 1804, while a second son, Thomas (1st), was born in 1806. In the parish records of christenings between 1840-51, there are registered the baptisms of nine children of Thomas (1st), carpenter, and Mary Anne Apps; Thomas (2nd) was christened in 1840. Mary Anne died in 1852. In the 1881 census, Thomas (2nd) Apps, aged 40,

with his wife, Caroline, is listed as a shipbuilder and lived in Shipyard House, probably the house now called "Hope Cottage". This Thomas (2nd) was a Deacon and a Sunday school teacher in the Congregational Church for over forty years. He was given the nickname of 'Gloria' for he was always singing the refrain from a hymn 'Glory, glory, Hallelujah'. The last of the big schooners built at this yard was The Good Hope of about 115 tons, which was launched in 1903 and christened with hop tea. She started her first voyage on 3rd May 1903. She was used for trading along the coast until 1916, when she was sunk by enemy action during the 1st World War. In 1924, this yard was sold to Spencer and Bryce who built smaller boats. This

Thomas Apps, one time owner of Apps Shipyard situated on the north side of Quay Meadow

1. Spencer & Brice bought the Apps Shipyard in 1924

2. A vessel believed to be the Good Hope, on the stocks of the Apps Shipyard, Quay Meadow, about 1900

3. Charlie Hickman, the blacksmith at Apps Shipyard. He married the boss's daughter, Edith Apps

4. A vessel thought to be the Dolly Varden, on the stocks of Smart's Yard on the High Path or Craut - now known as the Trippet. Kate Smart who married Fred Woods, leased the yard to Abraham Apps, a cousin of Thomas

104

yard closed at the outbreak of war in 1939.

Another yard was Smarts, who also built similar sized boats to the Quay Meadow yard but specialised more in fishing boats. In the Mercantile Navy List of 1878, Thomas Smart of Bosham was listed as being the owner of the 79-ton Schooner Nugget, a vessel photographed in Bosham on more than one occasion. It is not known where she was built but she was registered in Arundel. Kate Smart, who married Frederick Woods, the Captain of the Emily Annie, inherited the yard from her

themselves lived in Primrose Cottage, a few doors east of their boatyard.

In 1882, this yard built the two masted schooner The Two Sisters (124-tons) named after Kate Smart's two sisters as well as The Lady of the Lake (84-tons) and the Dolly Varden; the latter was probably the last of the large vessels built in this yard. Annie Hector, (sometimes known as 'Dolly') née Woods, a daughter of Kate Smart's, 'christened' (to use her own words) the Dolly Varden while Eva Duke recalled her excitement at being on board when she was launched. The family also had a

The Good Hope, a 115 ton schooner, built at and launched from the Apps Shipyard in 1903. She was sunk by enemy action in 1916

father, Thomas Smart, a shipwright. Kate later leased the yard to a cousin of Thomas Apps, Abraham Apps. This yard was on the High Path or Craut (now known as the Trippet) where a house called The Haven has since been built. The sea wall has been filled in where once there was a lifting bridge across the gap to allow for the launching of the newly constructed boats. The Smarts'

coalyard, four cottages in Mariners Terrace, 4, 5, and 6 Gloucester Terrace as well as Westbrook Field. Kate Smart herself owned a number of colliers which brought coal from Newcastle to Bosham Quay. Most of this property passed to Annie Hector, their only child, in 1929 on the death of Kate and Frederick Woods within a week of each other.

In 1906, Alex Fowler established a yard further along the High Path, Mariners'Yard, from where in 1922 was launched the 108ft. New Prince of Wales, which was built for the Southend Navigation Company. At the time she was the largest shallow-draft passenger vessel in the world. In order to conform to the then regulations, she had to be built under cover, so tin sheds were constructed. There were only about two tides a year high enough to enable her to be launched. On the appointed day, with a cameraman from the Daily Mirror, the Managing Director's wife, Mrs. Wade, broke the bottle of champagne hard against the bow and, according to Bogia Coombes, one of those who had been employed in her construction and present at the launching, 'she went out beautiful'. 'Too well', according to Bogia, for she went down the slipway with such verve that she grounded on the opposite shore. Never have a group of men sobered up or moved so fast as they successfully pushed her off from the shore on Gosportside opposite the yard. If they had not done so, the vessel would have been there for another six months before there would have been another suitable high tide to enable her to float. The tin sheds were burned down in 1969 after which the area was used for many years by John Mant for storing and repairing boats. Now four houses have been constructed on the site. The gravel path that runs across from Mariners'Yard to Gosportside was made by Alex Fowler as a short cut home for lunch, when the tide was suitable, to save him the long walk all around past the old school at the top of the creek.

In about 1923, Lt. Col. F.S. Burne bought Mariners'Yard, later purchasing land on the east side of Cut Mill Creek where he established Burne's Shipyard. Here he built first 12 foot National dinghies and later the Chichester Harbour 18 foot One-Design dinghies. During the 2nd World War this yard was used by the Admiralty for repairing small boats while in February, 1943, the Dorman Long Company took over the fields between Burne's and Apps yards. A large crane was erected on this site

The 79 ton schooner, Nugget, which according to the Mercantile Navy List of 1878, was owned by Thomas Smart.

1. *The new Prince of Wales. Launched in Bosham in 1922, it was claimed that she was the largest flat-bottomed passenger vessel in the world. She was built for the Southend Navigation Co. and plied the Thames for many years*

2. *The sheds constructed for the building of the Prince of Wales*

3. *Duck shooters returning with their bag*

and here were brought by lorry and cart from Bosham Station, hundreds of steel plates which were stacked, eye witnesses reported, to a height level with the church steeple. About 250 men were employed in bolting together these plates to make pontoons of every size which formed the bases for the Mulberry Harbours. These pontoons, towed over to the Normandy beaches, were to play such an important part in the D-Day landings in June 1944. A canteen and wooden huts for living quarters were built in Miller Browns' fields, where now, in part, is the Bosham Sailing Club's dinghy park and in the field to the north, while sailors were billeted in The Slip. The completed pontoons were floated and towed into various creeks around the harbour where work to create the type of pontoons that were required, i.e. 'conveyor', 'ballast', these words being painted on the sides. The articulated concrete blocks which were used for launching the sections can still be seen along the shore south of the old shipyard. There were also anti-aircraft guns placed on the Quay. At the time, everything was done with great secrecy and few people, particularly in Bosham, knew for what purpose the whole operation was being undertaken; the building of these pontoons played a vital part in the success of the Normandy landings. The Dormon Long Company left Bosham in June 1946.

In 1947 both Mariners and Burnes' yards were acquired by brothers, David and Bob Bowker who in 1952 added a knitwear factory to the boatyard. Here they made yachting clothing under the trade name of Rockall which was sold to some of the major London shops. Later Bob took over the Rockall clothing and sail making side of the business entirely and, in partnership with Stan Budd, moved this operation to purpose-built premises in Brooks Lane, Broadbridge. Recently, the Brook's Lane site was sold for housing and the firm has re-established itself in the Delling Lane Business Park.

In about 1949-50, the Bowker brothers sold the Mariners' Shipyard to a jeweller from London who bought Pedalo beach catamarans for renting out at seaside resorts along the south coast. During the winter months Mariners' yard was used to repair these pleasure craft.

At the Burne's yard, David Bowker, took over the operation of the yacht yard himself where he built South Coast One-Designs (SCODs), Dragons, X One-Designs (XODs), 5.5 metre and cruising yachts for the pleasure and racing fraternity. David Bowker's own Dragon Scampi built at Burne's, was shipped to Copenhagen in the Royal Yacht Britannia on the occasion in 1957 of a state visit to Denmark by HM The Queen and Prince Phillip. Also shipped was Prince Phillip's own boat Bluebottle as well as two other dragons, to compete in races against the Danes. David Bowker sold Burne's in 1967 to a London businessman, but the demand for wooden boats declined and the yard closed in the late 1970s. The area is now almost derelict.

Sometime after the 1st World War, the three Combes brothers, Henry, Ernest and Bobby, started a yard in Furzefield Creek, initially as a shingle yard. Until the 1930s they transported gravel from the Winner Bank at the entrance to Chichester Harbour, to various places around the harbour including Bosham, which could account for the large area of gravel at Street End. Some of it went to Chichester via the canal from Birdham. During the 2nd World War, a number of slipways were built at the yard to fulfil orders from the Admiralty for whalers and lifeboats. After the war, the yard developed an international reputation as repairers of wooden boats. After the death of Ernest Combes in 1982, the Combes family sold out to a retired Naval Captain, Bob Greenshields, who in 1990 sold out to publisher Andrew Isaac, who had kept his own boat in this yard for many years. Owners of boats were also able to winter store and maintain their own yachts in the yard. However, problems arose and the yard was forced to close in 1999.

The fame of the good quality high-yielding corn of the Bosham area, due to the above average sun hours and good soil, had been known since Roman times. From the 14th century, the farms in Bosham were largely owned by the Berkeley family with tenant farmers working the land. In the Bosham rent books from 1755-60, there are five farms listed, some of the names of which are still around today. The main crops in the 17th century were corn and wheat

South Coast One Designs (SCODs) being built in Burne's Shipyard

109

largely for export to Ireland and the Low Countries. In about 1808 across the Cut Mill Creek a 4.5 metres (about 15 ft) high and 500metres (about 150 yards) long embankment was built between Chidham and Quay Meadow and the area used for farming; indeed in 1825, the Lord of the Manor granted leases for the use of the reclaimed land for this purpose. About thirty years later, as a result of very high tides or a gale, maybe both, the sea broke through - for many years there were accounts of the ruins of farm buildings being seen at low tide in Cut Mill Creek. This area subsequently proved a very suitable site for the cultivation of oysters. In the 1920s it was still possible for carts to go back and forth to Chidham at low tide, in part along the old mud wall. In about 1930 the Cut Mill channel was deepened either by the Lord of the Manor or Burnes Shipyard, so it is now no longer possible to cross from Chidham to Bosham.

It was the Enclosure Act of 1801 that first empowered land to be enclosed; this action was not completed in Bosham until 1821 by a private act of Parliament. In 1834, there were eight hundred and thirty acres of enclosed land in the village. From then on land in Bosham was still owned principally by the two families - the Berkeleys and Cheesmans, the latter the lay rectors of the village. By 1919, the Berkeleys had sold the last of their land, mostly to their former tenants, which they had been doing slowly since about 1850. Old Park Farm, one of the farms mentioned in the Berkeley Castle rent book in 1759, was the last to be sold, when Edgar Berkeley, the 4th Baron Gifford sold, in 1919, the Manor of Bosham to Albert Eadie, the bicycle manufacturer.

One of the earlier families to come to Bosham was the Heaver family who arrived in 1850, when John Heaver farmed two hundred and fifty acres in the Broadbridge area. Only five years later he died leaving an 18-year-old son, also John, to continue to work on the farms: indeed in the 1899 Kelly's directory John is listed as farming at Broadbridge. This included Broadbridge Mill, which closed down in 1923. There is a bill of the Heavers' dated 25 July 1894 for threshing 25 sacks of oats at a cost £1.5s.0d. (£1.25p) With great ability and business acumen, the younger John increased his acreage, buying many of the smaller farms around so that by the early 1960s the descendants of the two John's had formed a flourishing family business under the name of Broadbridge Farms, cultivating more than one thousand acres. In the 1937 Kelly's Directory, Douglas Heaver is shown as farming Brooks Farm, Bullock Barn Farm and Broadbridge Farm. The family lived originally in Broadbridge House, which in 1939 on the outbreak of war, was commandeered by the army. The house was pulled down in 1945. On the land, sheep were grazed until the 1930s and there were also two large herds of Friesian and tubercular-tested Guernsey dairy herds. Broadbridge Farms formed Chichester Dairies, the second largest privately-owned dairy in UK, supplying milk not only in the West Sussex area,

1. The barn on Hoe Farm. A few weeks after this photograph was taken, the barn was destroyed in the 1987 hurricane

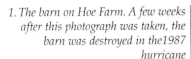

2. The slab at the corner of a ruined barn on Hoe Farm at the right height for the collection of milk churns by the daily lorries

3. Tom Coombes ploughing on Bosham Hoe in 1913

4. William Coward on top of a hayrick at Church Farm, Old Park Lane in the early 1920s

5. Thatching a hayrick at Rectory Farm

but also to London. The local dairy business declined and little of the milk sold in the village today comes from local herds..

At Ratham Mill, the last of of the five mills to operate on the Bosham stream and within the Heaver empire, was converted to electricity for grinding cereals for cattle feed. Another commodity was growing sixty acres of prime pea seeds for Birds Eye growers in the eastern counties of England for the canning and freezer markets. Another industry of the family was brick making

former farm buildings have been converted into a Business Park. All the present Heaver family still live within a four-mile radius of Bosham, but none in the village.

Another farming family, the last such family to reside in the village, were the Stranges when Joseph leased Harts Farm in 1896. He had four daughters and six sons - one by one he found farms to rent for each of his boys. In the Kelly's Directory of 1899, John Strange is listed as a farmer and horse breeder at Harts Farm, while Grove

Part of Joseph Strange's family of four sons & six daughters outside Hoe farm house before 1913

on the west side of Brooks Lane; this is now a large housing estate. Today the Heaver family, under the name of Heaver Farms Ltd, farm in excess of sixteen hundred acres in and around Bosham, given over to arable, while the

Doman Strange worked Park Farm. John Joseph's eldest son, George, rented Hoe Farm which at that time included one hundred and twenty seven acres of land on the present Hoe estate as well as twenty five acres around Hoe

Farmhouse, Hoe Lane, where the family lived. George Strange bought the farm in 1926 only to sell it within three years to buy the one hundred and twenty three acres of Rectory Farm, which included Walton Farm, from the last member of the Cheesman family . Until 1937, the Cheesmans had been the lay rectors of the village for many decades. Included in this purchase of the two farms were eleven houses as well as Rectory House. During the depression of the 1930s some of the houses had to be sold and this included Rectory House, while the family moved into the farm cottages nearby, which had been known as Burnt House, and renamed them Rectory Farm. George had married in 1912 Miller George Brown's daughter, Nellie; and their first-born son was Douglas. George Brown himself was involved in pig farming for Shippams to make their famous sausages. He kept the pigs in portable huts in the yard by the mill as well as at Hoe Farm. One elderly lady many years later was to comment that in her youth, Quay Meadow did not smell as sweet as it does today. The pigs were walked to East Street, Chichester for slaughtering at the Shippam factory.

With the declaration of war in 1939, farmers became a vital part of the economy of the country and locally were required to produce food to feed the growing numbers of men employed in the dockyards and servicemen based in the Portsmouth area. Food was rationed while milk, wheat, corn and potatoes were vital necessities for feeding the population.

So the farmers prospered.

With the end of the war, governments realised that a well-fed nation was a healthy one, so farmers were given subsidies to enable food to be sold cheaper than would otherwise be possible. At Bosham station, loading facilities were built for the transport of sugar beet to the East Coast processing factories, while tractors replaced horses and farmers employed fewer men. George Strange retired in 1947 and his son Douglas took over the running of the farms. One of the victims of the 'Beeching' railway cuts was the closure of the goods yards at Bosham which brought the growing of sugar beet in the area to an end. But otherwise life continued as before with farms having a balance of arable and livestock. Douglas became a first class farmer winning, amongst other competitions, one for the best farm of less than two hundred acres in the Chichester area as well as, in 1960, being the runner-up for producing the best sample of milling wheat in the UK. He was also a great horseman and was often seen riding around his land on one of his magnificent horses inspecting his animals and his fields, for at that time there were herds of cows on many of the Strange farms. Douglas died very suddenly in July 1993 and his son Richard, with his brother Alan, took over his father's interests in Bosham and enlarged them. With the closure of the Chichester cattle market, the ever-increasing regulations and paper work involved in farming livestock, in 1996 the family ceased farming cattle. John Joseph's great great-grandson, Richard's son Alastair, graduated in 2001 with a degree in agriculture and now works with his father, between them working twelve hundred acres of arable in Bosham, Cobnor, Thorney Island and Lavant.

In 1924 Sigmund Gestetner, son of the founder of the famous duplicating machinery company, arrived in Bosham with a friend for a sailing holiday. He fell in love with the area and so began his association with the village by renting Petworth Cottage, off Taylors Lane. Sigmund was later to buy the house which had been converted from two thatched cottages. (Petworth Cottage was to suffer from two serious fires in 1947 and 1982 and, as a result, has been almost completely rebuilt.) The Gestetner family bought a number of farms in the area, one of them being Southwood Farm which included a Grade II listed Georgian farmhouse, one of the farms recorded in the Berkeley Castle Bosham Rent Book of 1755. Here, by 1948, he had built up a prize herd of pedigree attested Ayrshires; he later changed to Friesians as they gave a higher milk yield. Before long the family owned a large proportion of the south-west area of Bosham to which was added the rearing and farming of chickens and pigs. There was also a family nursery (vegetable) garden, much of the produce winning prizes in the local horticultural society shows. In 1937, Sigmund purchased the house Four Winds on Shore Road, which during the 2nd World War was occupied

Sigmund Gestetner photographed outside his house, Petworth Cottage, in about 1946

by Field Marshall Lord Templar. After the war the house was used as a Kibbutz to train young people from inner cities such as Glasgow and Liverpool, to work on the land. The young people then went on to farm in Israel joining one of the Kibbutzim. This house was sold in 1960 but not before being let for some years to Marks and Spencer's for use as a rest home for their staff.

The dairies closed in 1991, when problems with milk quotas and European Union regulations made milk production uneconomic. Jonathan Bentall of Chidham now leases the Gestetner farmlands as well as fields belonging to other local landowners in the area, growing only arable crops. But the Gestetner family still retain many of the original farm cottages as well as Petworth Cottage. There is also a plan to convert two of the redundant 19th century threshing barns into residential dwellings, landscaping the surrounding area at the same time.

In 1933 Vic Baker took over the tenancy of the two hundred acre Church Farm in Old Park Lane bringing with him a small herd of cows, minimal machinery and two carthorses. To give one some idea of the state of farming at that time, he was allowed to occupy the farm rent-free for two years. In the early years at Church Farm he augmented his meagre income by the sale at Portsmouth market of rabbits and mushrooms, both of which were plentiful in this area. A shortage of water forced the sale of the cows within a year or two of his arrival – mains water and electricity did not arrive until the early 1950s. Instead he grew cereals, potatoes and sugar beet; the latter ceased when the goods yard at Bosham Station was closed.

Vic, together with his two sons, Julian and Brian, when they left school, started a turkey farm which thirty-seven years later was producing 100,000 birds a year. In 1992, Julian was joined by his son Matthew and the farm was further expanded. By 2000, competition from the continent which enabled European farmers to import turkeys at two thirds of the price of home-produced birds, proved too much and the turkey farm was forced to close. The barns that were used to fatten turkeys are now used for the leisure industry – for the storage of caravans and boats.

Brick and tile-making were another industry in Bosham for many hundreds of years, not surprisingly with so much clay soil in the area. The Romans brought the art of brick-making to this country - the practice was forgotten on their departure. It was not until the mid-15th century that brick making was brought back to this country by Flemish brick makers who, in 1440, built Herstmonceux Castle in East Sussex. In the early days when the bricks and tiles were moved by water, the three requirements for such works were clay, furze for fuelling the kilns and easy access to the sea. There are the remains of many Roman brickworks which fill these requirements around the harbour and one of these may well have been the one on Bosham Hoe. There is evidence that this brick and tile works were in operation at the end of the 15th century for the north-west shore of the oakwoods on the Hoe is littered with broken bricks and tiles. There were also two cottages used by the managers, on the ruins of which have now been built the houses known as Furzefield and Furzefield Cottage. Also there are the ruins of two kilns and the brick foundations of a 17th century building as well as two or three wells. One of the earliest recorded mention of the works is in a lease of 1759 between the 4th Earl of Berkeley and John Twine for twenty-three acres of pasture, a brick kiln and tilehouse at Furzefield. The first map record of a kiln was in those of 1813 and 1879.

Another brickworks was on the main Portsmouth road between Chequers and Walton Lanes, which had been owned by the Cheesman family. The buildings remaining are now used as offices by the Eric Brinkman Estates, where examples of the roofing tiles made at these works can still to be seen on the roofs of the remaining buildings. These brickworks were in existence in 1867 and closed during the 1st World War. The bricks made here from two of the kilns were used in the building of the Carmelite Convent at Hunston, just south of the Chichester By-pass (the

Above: Broken tiles & bricks on the shore at the northwest corner of Bosham Hoe. These are the remains of the brickworks - now demolished - which may well have been here since Roman times.
Left & inset: The roof of the former Cheeseman brickworks on the main road showing various styles of roof tiling produced by the company

A27 trunk road). In 1930, Eric Brinkman remembers as a child seeing the remains of kilns twelve feet (about 3.6 meters) deep, built in the shape of a pyramid with no lid. There were two other brickfields, one south of Colner Farm and the other on the west side of Brooks Lane at Broadbridge, both advertised by John W. T. Heaver between 1913 and 1918. The Colner one was closed in 1918 while the Broadbridge one operated until 1930. In the 1830s there was an annual cricket match between the brickyards' employees of the Walton and Hoe yards versus the local farm workers. The game was played in the meadow behind Strange Hall.

Timber was the third most important export from the Sussex coasts at the time of Elizabeth I, the removal of which caused a great deal of erosion and subsequent silting of Sussex harbours. Bosham, with large areas of oak woods, no doubt benefited from this export. Douglas Strange wrote of oak trees that were taken from Upper Wolves Copse, Bosham Hoe, during the 1914 war and put on the railway at Bosham for use in the war-making machinery

The trade of forging metal must go back to the Iron Age. The Romans brought the art to Britain and some of their metal work can be seen at the Fishbourne Roman Palace. So it would be surprising if there were not blacksmiths in Bosham from that period. They would have been needed for making nails by the thousands for new buildings and agricultural implements like ploughs and cartwheels. In the 17th century, from inventories and wills it has been ascertained that there were four blacksmiths in Bosham at that time. By the 19th century, there were two forges operating here - five generations of the Redman family worked at the forge sited next door to Laurel Cottage in Walton Lane as well as at another forge on the main road at Fishbourne, at the time within the Parish of Bosham. The forge at Fishbourne had, as a regular customer, Lord Gifford of Old Park. An account from the Redman's of 1894 shows that Lord Gifford was charged two shillings (10p.) for 'cutting down two horses' feet' as well as three shillings and sixpence (17.5p) 'for four shoes for a filly'.

While the Redman family had worked hard all through the 2nd World War repairing agricultural machinery and shoeing horses, after the war with wholesale mechanisation, the blacksmiths and farriers found themselves with less and less work. George Redman did make a few pieces of ornamental ironwork but orders were insufficient to keep the family financially above water. George designed and made with the help of his son, John, the gates at the entrance to the house The Town Hall on the Trippet as well as the gates at the entrance to Church Path in memory of Sir Hugh Allen. The Bosham forge closed in 1982 and, sadly, as no further use could be found for this old workshop the building was pulled down. A private house has been built on the site but some of the tools from the forge went to the Weald and Downland

Open Air Museum at Singleton.

The other forge in the village was attached to the Apps Shipyard on Quay Meadow. This one did work for private individuals but was basically used by the yard for the shipbuilding. One of the last blacksmiths there was Charlie Hickman, son-in-law of Thomas Apps, the owners of the yard.

There were many other trades that had workers in the village; amongst them were carpenters, bricklayers, stonemasons, milliners, dressmakers, tailors and shoemakers. By the late 19th century housewives were able to go to Chichester and other local towns to buy their pots and pans, their clothing and their furniture, so local craftsmen were no longer able to make a living locally.

Today there are few of the old industries operating in the village, but new ones have arrived so the former Broadbridge Farm buildings have been converted to other uses. There is now a Farm Shop to which the Bosham Station Post Office moved in April, 1998, a cake making factory, a doctors' surgery, sail makers and many other small enterprises, utilising these buildings. No longer can people set up small industries in the backyard of their private houses, for areas are now designated for business or residential use. Industries have to seek planning permission before doing anything which results in a change of usage or alterations to buildings within this Area of Outstanding Natural Beauty.

Norman Redman and his son shoeing a horse outside their forge in Walton Lane

CHAPTER 10

Always Learning Many Things Plutarch

It was the ecclesiastical foundations that first instituted small schools to teach young boys, bound for the priesthood, the basic skills of reading and writing as well as the important subject of Latin, the language of the Church. There may have been one attached to the college in Bosham run by the Austin Canons who, after 1120, occupied the area south of the church. This school, if there was one, would have disappeared with the Dissolution of the Monasteries. Under two George Parker bequests, there were two schoolmasters appointed in Bosham, in 1558 and 1762, while, in 1765, a schoolmistress was appointed! In 1775 the curate, John Gregory taught 'by licence'. One cannot but wonder where he taught – probably in the church - and who were his pupils?

From the records available today, in 1812 the first official school was opened in Bosham, when the group that had broken away from the Established Church to form the Union Chapel and who held their services in the oyster barn on Shore Road, started a Sunday School. In 1875, a schoolroom was built next door to the Congregational Church, now the United Reformed Church hall in Bosham Lane. The thatched cottage next door was occupied for sixty years by William Norris, the Sunday School

The old school, a National School, opened in 1834 at the top of School Rithe

teacher who was also the chapel keeper and the village carrier.

The first full time school, the National School, was opened in 1834 in a purpose built schoolhouse at the top of School Rithe on land given by Captain Maurice Berkeley, Royal Navy, the Lord of the Manor. Captain Berkeley also promised an annual subscription of £10 a year while ninety-six parents pledged a penny per week, some double that amount. The money raised for the cost of the building was due to the energies of the then curate, the Rev. George Augustus How, who donated £5, while the National Society for the Education of the Poor in the Principles of the Established Church donated £100. The Treasury gave £90, a grant that had been available to all new schools since 1833, while the Bishop, Dean and Chapter of Chichester donated £65. The National Society had been set up to provide voluntary schools following the principles of the Church of England. There were two rooms in the building, 9.2 x 5.2m.(30 x 17 feet) each of which accommodated sixty boys and sixty girls and in which lessons were held five and a half days a week with Sunday school on Sunday afternoon.

The building is still there, but is now a private house. It was some way from the centre of the village, but this may have been because a large number of the pupils lived either on Gosportside or in the outlying districts of Hook, the Hoe and Lower Hone, or perhaps just because the land had been a gift. However, this had its disadvantages; in the school record books of the time, there are frequent references to the school being closed because high tides and strong winds, even heavy snowfalls, made it difficult for the children to reach the building. Eva Purser recalled that

The senior class of the Bosham Board School in 1897

120

when lessons began or finished at the time of high tides, the boys of the school were required to take the school benches down to the Critchfield Stream, the waterway that flows down from Critchfield Road to the sea about forty yards (39 metres) north west of the schoolhouse, over which the girl pupils would walk to prevent the hems of their dresses getting wet. In 1895, an embankment was built in front of the school building. Before that the school had been completely surrounded by seawater at times of high spring tides,

In 1893, the Bosham School Board was set up, with the vicar of the parish at the time as Chairman of the Board and the school was renamed the Bosham Board School. In the record books, the signature of the vicar, the Rev. Henry Mitchell, occurs frequently under the words 'checked the Registers and found them correct; attendance excellent. Signed Henry Mitchell, Chairman.'

The local farmers, most of them illiterate, were not too happy at this new school, for they foresaw their workforce being better educated than they were; this in their view might produce complications. The first master and mistress were appointed in 1835 on a joint salary of £40 a year. The school was regularly closed for such things as Regatta Day, Foresters' Fête, Church Fête, school treat, 'for use as a Polling Station for Parish Council elections' and 'for a clothing club to be held on the premises'. An entry for the 4th June 1895 reads 'School closed on Tuesday after only forty seven children presented themselves in the afternoon'. Apparently the children were needed to help with the harvesting while on 31st October 'owing to heavy rains only forty eight children presented themselves out

The new Bosham Board School the year it was opened in 1896

of one hundred and eighty two'. It was usually the headmaster who maintained the reports in the record books.

After fifty two years, the 1834 building was proving insufficient to hold all the children and there were frequent references to flooding and buildings being damaged by water. An entry for 6th November 1895 reads, 'The approaches to the W.C.s [toilets] are flooded and the children cannot go to them without wetting their feet'. In 1896 a new school was built in Walton Lane for two hundred and twenty children to be called the Bosham Board School. The record book entry for 8th June 1896 is 'school closed'. For the 9th June 1896 'Opened school in new buildings this afternoon'. If there was an official opening of the new building, the headmaster makes no reference to it.

The school weathervane first used in1834 and on every school since

Adjacent to the new school, a house was built for the schoolmaster, both buildings financed by a charge on the rates. The weather vane, which had been on the original school building, was moved to the new one and has continued to be a landmark in the village, for it is now on the roof of the newest school building of 1977. The Master, William Alfred Scales who with his wife, Sissie, as Mistress, continued as the headmaster until he retired in 1923. Also a teacher in the school was Alice Layzell, wife of Ernest Layzell, the baker, and mother of Eva Purser, a pupil of the old and new schools.

Half holidays were given frequently for all manner of events. On May 21st 1898, 'half holiday was given today to celebrate the relief of Mafeking [famous battle of the Boer War in South Africa] after [headmaster] giving a short history of the siege, the children gave three cheers for Col. Baden Powell, Col. Plummer and General Roberts and sang God Save the Queen' [Queen Victoria], while on 1st February, 1901, the school was closed on account of Queen Victoria's funeral. Empire Day on May 25th was also celebrated each year. In 1908, the entry reads 'Lessons on our Empire were given to each class at 11.30. God save the King [Edward VII] was sung, the boys saluting the King's picture having no flag' Even with the new buildings, there were frequent problems. Entries such as 'no fire on account of water in the stoke hole. Temp of school 48°F'; 'Temp at opening of school 35°F no fire'; 'For some time past I have complained without effect of the bad drainage in the playground. The stoke hole of the heating apparatus is now constantly flooded.....no managers now appear to take any interest in the school'.

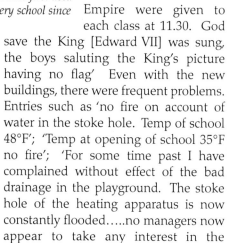

It would appear that even then parents could be difficult. On October 15th 1906 the record reads 'Mrs. Bignell visited the school on Monday 8th in reference to her boy leaving school and his being punished. I told her the boy must obey the rules of the school and discipline must be maintained, she said she would allow no one to punish her children'.

In 1909 the school was enlarged to accommodate another one hundred pupils, which gives some idea of the size of the village at that time. Even after the enlargement of the school, there was still an entry in July 1910 'Copy of HM Inspector's report on "Premises". 1. The Offices are sufficient and suitable but owing to the cesspit having become full to overflowing they are at present in a deplorable state and dangerous to health. If the cesspit cannot be emptied without delay the school should be closed. 2. The playgrounds are badly drained and ….. 3. There is no water on the Premises either for the Teacher's house or the school……' In September 1918 (which would have been during the 1st World War), the school was closed for two days for blackberrying.

In the 1901 census, William Scales, aged 42, is listed as the schoolmaster with three sons and three daughters. One son, Clifford, then aged eight, was in September 1909 appointed a student teacher. In 1923, Clifford became headmaster, taking over from his father. When in 1952, Clifford retired father and son had been headmasters in the school for a total of sixty-two years.

Again, according to the record books, the school was frequently closed, in some cases for three weeks at a time, owing to outbreaks of mumps, chicken pox, scarlet fever and diphtheria.

In March 1973 as a result of the inspection of the roof structure and the wall in the centre of the main building, the school was considered unsafe. Within four days, alternative temporary school accommodation was found for the senior children at the Parklands [Chichester] County Primary School and for the juniors in the old Fishbourne School while repairs were made to the school building. Even with all these remedial repairs, by 1977 the building was once again found to be unsafe. A new larger school building was erected on the same site, so for a whole year the pupils were taught in 'Portacabins' erected on the Parish Recreation Ground, the village hall was used as an assembly and dining room and the village hall car park used as the school playground. This school, now named the Bosham Primary School, is today a flourishing well run school with around two hundred pupils. Between 2003 and 2004, six of the seven class rooms were extended and a sensory room was added for children with learning difficulties.

For over thirty years, there has been a very well run playgroup operating at St. Nicholas Hall, Broadbridge, for five mornings a week. Here about twenty-seven children between the ages of two and five are organised by five fully qualified staff. While the parents have to pay a small fee, those children over three years of age are partly funded by the West Sussex authorities.

There is also the Ladybird Montessori School which uses the function room of the new village hall in Walton Lane as a schoolroom. Here, for five mornings and two afternoons a week, a maximum of sixteen children are taught by the method of teaching invented by Maria Montessori whereby young children are 'allowed to learn at their own pace without pressure....' Again the school is part government funded and there is usually a waiting list.

At the beginning of the 20th century, there were also two Dame's schools in the area – that is a private school usually run by a mature matron-type figure. For many years, Rosie Frogbrooke's grandmother (see Chapter 11) ran a school in the house next door to Galleon House in the High Street, the building then known as the School House. This building has since been pulled down and replaced by a garage. There was another Dame's school at Home Farm on the main road in what is now the village of Fishbourne, a house at right angles to the road by the de-restriction sign. Here Eva Purser's mother, Alice Layzell, the baker's wife, also taught for a while.

As the village expands and more houses are built and occupied by young couples with school aged children, one can expect an increasing demand for more and more facilities for kindergarten and primary school children. Today, most of the children from the Bosham Primary School go on to secondary schools in Chichester and Portsmouth, the latter just a short train ride from Bosham.

The Bosham primary school of 1978 with the weathervane on top of the building to the right

CHAPTER 11

The Folk that made the Village

Augustus Hare wrote in his book on Sussex in 1894, 'Sussex has many advantages, but its greatest admirers will not claim that the population is endowed with good looks. The people of Bosham, however, are remarkably handsome. It has a well-to-do fishing population of evident foreign extraction, who stand aloof from their neighbours, seldom marry out of the place, and keep their good looks to themselves'. With vessels frequenting the port over many centuries, no one need be surprised that the seed of many European seafarers was sown in the village, for until the arrival of the trains in 1846, the girls of the village would have had only local men from whom to choose a husband. One only has to look through the marriages and baptisms in the church records to see how much intermarriage there has been between

The School House in the High Street, where William and Charlotte Frogbrook lived and where Charlotte had a school

125

the local families.

There are some families that have been a part of the local scene for hundreds of years, others that have come and gone but have nevertheless left their mark on the village. From the oldest families come such names as John Frogbrook who married in Bosham in 1604; Francis Kervill believed to be from Normandy, who married a Bosham girl in 1693; Edmond Bennett Martin, who married in Bosham parish church in 1761, and the Arnolds, the first recorded of these being one of the men whose name appeared in the Bosham Protestation of 1641. Some of these names still appear in the church records today. Of the more recent arrivals have been the Combes, the Gilbys, and the Stranges.

To start with the Frogbrooks, the origin of this name is supposed to go back to the 17th century, when a local vicar and his wife, hearing crying during the night, found a baby hidden in the rushes by the brook. As the vicar had no children and the mother of the baby could not be found, he and his wife adopted the foundling and brought him up as their own, calling him John Frogbrook - the foundling (frog) found in the brook. The baby was alleged to be the illegitimate child of a local noble lady about to marry an equally noble gentleman - her name has been lost in the mists of time but there has been a Frogbrook named John in almost every generation since.

A descendant of John, William Frogbrook, born in 1841, was parish clerk and sexton as well as bailiff of the manor, quaymaster and coroner's official. He married Charlotte Moore and lived in The School House, a thatched house on the corner of the High Street opposite the church and next door to the sweetshop, now Galleon House. William and Charlotte were to have fourteen children over a period of nineteen years, the eldest of whom was Ethel. Charlotte was the teacher at this fee-paying school, otherwise known as a Dame's School, which she ran with Miss Mitchell, the vicar's daughter. On one occasion Charlotte took her young daughter, Ethel, into the tunnel under The School House which ran between the church and The Anchor. The little girl broke off a small piece of stalactite from the wall; afterwards when describing the event she said she felt as if she had gone into a

Captain Ernie Frogbrook with his dog in the 1930s

room of diamonds, for the stalactite glistened in the dampness. Ethel was told by her mother that the tunnel was supposed to run to the Manor House and up to the main road. There is evidence of such a tunnel, for when workmen digging drains or the like in the gardens of houses fronting on to the west side of Bosham Lane, they broke into what appeared to be a tunnel running north-south.

Lord Gifford, Lord of the Manor, used Bill, as he called William Frogbrook, as his right hand man. Sadly, in January 1911 William died, the same year as Lord Gifford; a month later his son, Sydney William, was appointed Harbour Master of the Port of Bosham. In 1899, another member of the family, Edmund Frogbrook, became captain of the 2nd Lord Iveagh's yachts, twenty five years before Lord Iveagh became Lord of the Manor of Bosham. Ethel, with the help of two of her daughters, Rosie and Nora, ran a guesthouse in what had been The Gloucester Inn. A later member of the Frogbrook family, Frank, born in 1878, ran a very successful lacemaking business in London where the lace for the wedding dress of Queen Elizabeth II was made. This business was closed in 1956. His brother Cecil Edward Frogbrook was a master tailor also working in London who, when he retired, returned to Bosham and was buried here in 1934. The last of the Bosham Frogbrooks, Harold, died in 2002 and he too is buried here.

Another family which occupied the position of parish clerk over many generations were the Kearvells. The family probably originated in Brittany or Normandy and settled in Sussex when, in 1693, Francis Kervil married Elizabeth Cupin (1671 - 1707), the youngest daughter of Stephen and Rose Cupin of Bosham. Kervil was an old Norman name but over the centuries has been spelt in many different ways. With few people able to read or write, it was the written interpretation of the pronunciation of the name as given to the vicar or curate signing the baptism, wedding or death certificates that accounts for the many different spellings. There was Kearvel, Kervel, Karvil, Kervell, Kearvele, Kearvil, Kervele, Kervil, in all nineteen variations when finally in about 1840 it was established as Kearvell. In spite of the various forms of the spelling of this surname, all can be traced back to Francis and Elizabeth. Many generations of the family were master craftsmen, usually of wood, being carpenters, joiners and wheelwrights, forming successful enterprises and employing many craftsmen. John Kearvell (1787–1868) made some of the pews that are near the front of the church, where his initials and the date, 1845, have been carved under the seats. In 1841, John successfully tendered for the job of repairing the church tower and spire, amounting to £220 5s 8d (approximately £220.28p) which had to be paid to him in instalments owing to the shortage of cash in the church funds.

However, the Kearvell name is famous for another story, which has been written up by many people each

127

with a slightly different twist. Tom Kearvell (1763-1830) was parish clerk and after his death his son, also Tom (1789-1865), took over his father's duties. C.J Longcroft, in his book on Bosham written in 1867, recounts the story of how, during the time when William Killick was Vicar of Bosham (1800-38), the parish records were destroyed by a Tom Kearvel. Killick was a very sociable man, enjoying wining and dining, while largely neglecting his duties as parish priest. He was proud of the parish records and regularly had the parish clerk, Tom, called out from the pub, usually on Saturday nights, to fetch these records from the old 13th century chest in the church and to take them to the vicarage to be shown to the guests. Tom was then expected to wait in the kitchen of the vicarage until the vicar was ready for Tom to return them to the church. On this particularly occasion, Tom snapped! It was a snowy cold Saturday evening, two days before Christmas. Instead of returning the papers to the chest, so the story goes, he burned the lot on a bonfire. Saturday 23rd December occurred only five times in the first half of the 19th century - 1809, 1815, 1820, 1826 and 1837; so the incident would have been within living memory of some of those living in 1867, when Longcroft's book was published. The story is repeated by Kenneth MacDermott, vicar of Bosham 1902-15, in his book of 1911 when he wrote 'There is a story....which we believe to be in the main true, though the destruction of the old books, &c., was certainly not so complete as Mr.

Longcroft makes out'. But none of the parish records is missing! So whichever of the Kearvell parish clerks did this terrible deed, what records did he burn?

There is another account of this incident given by members of the Kearvell family. The second Tom Kearvell, parish clerk, had a sister, Jane, who never married but had three illegitimate sons by a local man, Henry Hammond, a deserter from the Navy. Should Henry have been caught by the authorities, he would have been sentenced to death for desertion. Did Henry Hammond destroy the bastardy records and assume, together with his three illegitimate sons, Jane's surname of Kearvell in order to conceal his identity? The plot deepens further, for in May 2001, a letter dated September 1845, written by a J.B. Freeland, was found among some legal documents in the West Sussex Records Office. This letter gives an account as recorded by Alexander Hay, when Hay was collecting material for a history of Bosham he was writing. He wrote of how the parish clerk of Bosham burnt the charters and parish documents. Hay died on 15th November 1806, so if this letter is an accurate record, it suggests that the incident occurred between 1800, when Killick arrived in Bosham, and 1806, when Hay died. But in these six years, there was no December 23rd on a Saturday. Descendants of the illegitimate sons of Jane, Henry Hammond Kearvell born 18th January, 1829, and George Hammond Kearvell, born 4th September 1831, are of the opinion that the event took place in 1837, when Jane's brother, Tom, was parish clerk and that it was the very old charters of Bosham, probably going back to the 13th century, that were destroyed. None of these old charters has ever been found. There are still Kearvells living in Bosham today.

Until 1937 many generations of a yeoman farming family, the Cheesman's, were chamberlains and coroners of the Manor and Hundred of Bosham. In addition, some members of this family were the lay rectors for the church, their duties being to collect the tithes of the parish which were stored in a barn at Rectory Farm. This office was taken over by the Church Commissioners in 1937. The Cheesman family lived in Rectory House, which today is called Strange Hall, until it was sold by the executors of Alfred Cheesman in 1927. Charles Cheesman who died in 1849, had three illegitimate sons by Charlotte Kervele: Mark, baptised in 1813, Roger in 1815 and Alfred in 1823. Charles had an earlier illegitimate son, George, by Ann Masters of Chidham, who was christened in 1811. Charlotte Kervele and her sister Jane were the daughters of the supposed arsonist, Tom Kervele, and sisters of the other suspect, also Tom. In the census returns for 1861 and 1871, Charlotte is shown as living with her son Alfred at Rectory Farm. The Cheesman family have a vault beneath the chancel in the church where many of the family are buried. In the chancel there are also memorial windows to Charles, his son Alfred and his first wife

Caroline (1825-58) By his second wife, Elizabeth Amelia, Alfred had three more children, Charles Christopher Barwell baptised 1862, Alfred Hunter in 1865 and Mabel Elizabeth in 1869. Alfred Hunter took Holy Orders, became Vicar of Twigworth and Honorary Canon of Gloucester Cathedral. He died in 1941 and is buried at Twigworth next to his mother, Elizabeth Amelia, who died in 1917. Charles Christopher was the last Lay Rector of Bosham and when that office ceased in about 1927, he sold Strange Hall to the Strange family.

At the sale of furniture at Strange Hall in 1927, it is interesting to read the sums given for various items – a cottage piano in a rosewood case fetched £5 while a 5ft. 6ins. (1.69 metre) antique Sheraton bow-fronted sideboard fetched £26.9s.10d. (just under £26.50) The last of the Cheesman's, Charles Christopher Barwell Cheesman died in 1946 aged 84 in a building known as "The Hut", situated beside Burne's shipyard off Cut Mill Creek.

Although there is a possibility that there were members of the Martin family in Bosham in the 16th century, it was not until the 18th century that a direct line for this family was proved, when Mercy Bennett was married in Bosham in 1761 to Edmund Martin, a yeoman farmer. Edmund and Mercy had thirteen children in twenty-three years. Mercy was obviously made of stern stuff for she lived to the ripe old age of 85 in spite of bearing so many children. Both Edmund and his father were active in local life, being at various times churchwardens and overseers of the poor. One of their sons, Edward Bennett Martin, married into another local family with his marriage in 1802 to Anne Farndell and had nine children. Their eldest son, John born in 1803, became a pilot for ships entering Chichester Harbour, before taking over as landlord of The Berkeley Arms, combining this with the job of Bosham Quaymaster. For the lease of the quay he paid the Lord of the Manor £20 a year but he in turn was entitled to collect the tolls on any merchandise unloaded at the quay.

John married Patience Savage and also had nine children, three of whom became well-known characters in the village. Patience, after she was widowed, ran the sweetshop at the end

Robert Martin, brother of John, who leased the Quay in 1857

of the High Street - the house now called Galleon House. She also had a vessel named after her. Their son, also John, born in 1837, as well as being a ship owner became the landlord of The Anchor in the High Street, while his brother, Robert, who was also a master mariner, became the landlord of The Ship, two doors down from his brother. Robert married Emma Elizabeth Apps of the local ship building family. The third brother, George, born in 1841, also became a master mariner and shipowner, as well as skipper of the Thetis owned by Mr. Gatehouse of Broadbridge Mill. George caused quite a stir in the village when he eloped with the then vicar's daughter, Charlotte Sophia Mitchell. They were married in St. Mark's Church, Woolston, near Southampton, in July 1872 where two of their children were born. They then returned to Bosham where two more children were born and lived in various houses: in 1881 in the Hermitage, in 1891 Westbrook House and in the 1901 census in Riverside, Bosham Lane, where George is said to have ended his days. Here, after the death of his wife, he was cared for by his daughter Nora. One of those who helped with the plans for the runaway marriage was Ernest Layzell, a nephew of Frances Martin and a sister of the three brothers, for Frances had married Edward Layzell, a grocer, in about the 1870s. Ernest helped them carry their suitcases up to Cut Mill, where he had arranged a carriage to take them to Woolston for their marriage a few days later.

Two members of the Martin family

married into local families; Richard Frogbrook married Frances Emma Martin, daughter of John Martin of The Anchor in 1888, while Emma's brother, Allan 'Hearty' Martin, married Mary Louise Frogbrook in 1896.

In 1880, Ernest Layzell married Alice Purver, the daughter of George and Sarah Purver, who were the village bakers in the house then called Rose Cottage, on the corner of Critchfield Road and Bosham Lane, now the private house called Loafers. It had been the practice when a Bosham girl of good reputation got married, as she left the church on the arm of her new husband, to be given a gun salute fired from Quay Meadow. Alice Purver was the last bride to receive this honour. Ernest and Alice were to have three daughters, the eldest of whom was Eva Emily. It was Eva, born in 1886, who has left a wonderful account of her family and of life in Bosham at the end of the 19th and early 20th centuries. In one account she recalled her mother telling her of how in her childhood, when the Manor House was a farmhouse, she remembered the tenant Farmer Jenkins, always wearing a smock in the old tradition. Eva also remembered, swimming in Cut Mill Creek and changing into her bathing suit in the ruins of the old windmill after which the area was subsequently named - Windmill Fields. Eva's son, Stanley Purser, became an architectural draughtsman with a local firm of architects and amongst his jobs was that of regularly inspecting the fabric of

George Martin, brother of John & Robert, who eloped with the vicar's daughter. Here with his daughter Nora (& grand daughter) in the garden of Riverside, Bosham Lane

Bosham church.

After the death of George Purver, Sarah continued the business with the help of her son-in-law, Ernest Layzell.However,after three years the business was sold, Ernest returned to work for the railways and his wife, Alice, went to teach at the National School (see Chapters 9 & 12).

Purvers and Layzells seem to have disappeared from the Bosham scene, but the Martins continued to wield their influence locally. Edwin Cecil Martin, always known as Doodge, the grandson of Harry, another son of John and Patience, also followed the family custom of going to sea and usually lived on his own boat As a 'Man of Bosham', details of which can be found elsewhere in this book, he considered he could operate a repair business from his boat,

The Invader. He kept her tied to the piles by the quay, without paying tolls to the Lord of the Manor, at the time the 2nd Lord Iveagh. Lord Iveagh took Doodge to the High Court and the verdict went against Doodge who was forced to pay thereafter a regular charge to the Lord of the Manor. Doodge also captained the last of the trading vessels, the three-masted schooner, Kathleen and May, built in Clwyd in 1900, which was in the harbour for many years and is now in the care of the Maritime Trust. Although there is a descendant of Patience and John still living in the village, Doodge was the last of the seagoing Martins. David Martin, a great-grandson of Robert Martin, turned to banking and in the 1950s managed a branch of Barclays Bank two mornings a week in a room at the house called

The Windmill beside Cut Mill Creek. It was for this mill that the houses now built nearby were called Windmill Fields

Glenco, next to the then grocer's shop, Broadbridge's in Bosham Lane. He came by bus from Chichester with the necessary cash for the day's work in a black leather bag. When David retired from the bank, he bought a house at Berrymeads on the Main Road and took up market gardening and picture framing. Although David has three sons, none is inclined to earn his living as a seafarer, nor do any of them live in Bosham.

O f the Arnold family, the most famous was 'Grandsire' Arnold. Born in 1819, he became a choirboy at the age of ten, to become

Grandsire Arnold & his wife outside their cottage

the oldest and longest-serving chorister in England, singing almost to the day he died in 1912, aged 93. He married, in 1843, Eliza Stoveld, the daughter of a fisherman and lived in a thatched house on the 'High Path' or 'Craut' (a path now known as the Trippet) and had four sons. The eldest was Brigham, named after Brigham Young, one of the founders of the Mormon Church, his father being a follower of that sect. Grandsire's grandson, Robert, sailed in such famous yachts as Water Witch, Shamrock, White Heath and Sir Lipton, owned at one time by King George V. Robert married a Scottish girl, Margaret McKay, from Troon in Scotland in 1909 and lived in Myrtle Cottage in Mariners

Carlie (George Stoveld), otherwise known as Golden Toes, as he kept his sovereigns in the toe of his shoe for safety

Terrace, Bosham. Meg, as she became known, was surprised that in Bosham it was unfashionable to have lace curtains in the windows so she had to send to Scotland for some for her own windows. The other half of Myrtle Cottage was occupied by George Stoveld, otherwise known as 'Golden Toes' as he kept his sovereigns in the toes of his boots for safety! It was his widow, left with a son and a daughter to bring up, who ran the sweetshop in the High Street, after her husband was drowned. Mabel Stoveld, the unmarried daughter, continued to live in one half of the house until her death in 1991.

Another longstanding family in Bosham were the Collins' whose tombstones line the path to the entrance to Bosham church and include those of John and Amelia Collins, he having been a local farmer. The eldest of their ten children, also called Amelia, was born in Bosham in 1798. Amelia was a girl of great beauty and found herself in London when she was eighteen. There are two versions of how she arrived there. One was that, working in a Chichester draper's shop, Charges, where it is recorded that she was paid 1s. 9d. (about 6p.) a week, she eloped with an officer named Bennett of the Royal Sussex Regiment stationed in Chichester, who was possibly her cousin. The other story was that she was in service locally as a lady's maid and was taken by her employer to their London house. Whichever version is true, in 1819, Amelia married one George Idle in St. Martin-in-the Field, Trafalgar Square. He was the son of Christopher Idle, wine merchant and MP for Weymouth. The newlyweds settled in Paris near George's friend and fellow undergraduate at Oxford, Lord Yarmouth, later to become the 4th

Mr & Mrs Harry Collins & family. Harry Collins was the Postmaster, and was followed in due course by his elder son, also Harry, here standing between his parents

134

Marquess of Hertford. Seven years later George died, but Amelia stayed on in this select area of Paris, living only a few minutes away by carriage from Lord Yarmouth. She was paid an annual allowance of £1,000 from the Hertford estate. Twelve years after George died, Lord Yarmouth wrote a Will giving Amelia an annuity of £12,000 a year during her lifetime. After the fourth Marquess's death, this annuity, was paid half-yearly to Madame Idle by Richard Wallace, founder of the Wallace Collection in London, an illegitimate son of the Marquess and, it is thought, Amelia, though he was born before the Idles were married. Richard Wallace was prominent at the auction of her effects at Shopwhyke Hall after her death and bid for many of the items.

In 1861, Madame Idle, while retaining her apartment in Paris, returned to Bosham and rented Church Farm House, Bosham Lane, opposite what is now the Millstream Hotel, from Mr John Trevett, senior, for 10s. 8d. (just over 50p.). Here Francis Layzell supplied her with hand embroidered antimacassars. Amelia also set her mother up in Critchfield House, another 17th century house also in Bosham Lane, a few yards down from the farmhouse. Sometime after 1871 Amelia moved to Shopwhyke Hall, Oving, two miles east of Chichester, where she died in 1879 'of natural decay' according to her death certificate. Madame Idle never forgot her family and after she moved to Shopwhyke Hall used to send her carriage over to Bosham to have all the members of her

family, in turn, to tea on Thursday afternoons, (half day closing for the shops) where there was always a present for each one of them. The younger members of the family were not as appreciative of her generosity as they might have been, for they were expected to dress in their very best and behave perfectly while with Aunt Amelia, who comes over as a generous and friendly aunt but a stickler for good behaviour. During her lifetime, she was a munificent benefactor of many good works; she also gave a number of cups for boat racing by Bosham mariners and to individuals for competitions held by

Madame Idle, born Amelia Collins, who became the mistress of the Marquis of Hertford

the Royal Sussex Regiment. She was one of the donors for the building of Portfield church in Chichester, in the graveyard of which she is buried. She also left £1,000 to the Chichester Infirmary, afterwards named the Royal West Sussex Hospital.

During her lifetime, Amelia provided most of the members of her family with their own houses: those not provided for before her death were to have a share in the £60,000 that she left in her will. Today, the descendants of her brothers and sisters believe that, because the family was so diverse, some settling in Canada and Australia, the executors did not distribute all the estate for fear that yet another member of her family might appear and demand a share. Therefore, in some hidden account of some bank, there are millions of pounds accruing which have never been distributed. Harry Collins, the first postmaster of Bosham was one of her nephews and his house, now called Berkeley Cottage in Bosham Lane, was a gift from Amelia. Another great niece of Amelia married Ted Holden and had a house in the area that is now known as The Holdens, named after this family. Crede Cottage and Redfern House, where Gertie Collins lived, were two more of the houses she purchased for her family. Of Amelia's two brothers, Thomas became

The Iona alongside the quay in 1898. The third from the left is Grandpa Gilby, with another member of the Gilby family behind him

1 George Brown, the miller, & his wife Ida with their son Charles

2. Mr & Mrs John Joseph Strange in Hoe Lane

3. Mr & Mrs Strange with their six sons & four daughters

4. Dorothy Strange in front of Rectory Farm (formerly Burnt House) in 1933. The buildings started life in the 17th century as cottages

the publican of The Berkeley Arms and William of The Swan, while in the 1881 census, Edward Collins was the innkeeper of The Gloucester. Her two sisters, Jane Turner, who was with her when she died, and Ann Arnell each had a house at Chidham. Amelia's ghost is said to live on in many of the places in which she lived or stayed - at Shopwhyke Hall subsequent owners have claimed to have seen her as well as at Loafers in Bosham Lane, the former bakery run by the Layzell family.

Of the more recent arrivals in Bosham were the two Gilby brothers who arrived from Essex in 1850. While Jefferson Thomas joined the Navy, John Henry married, in 1857, a Bosham girl, Eliza Collins, when she was only seventeen, one of Amelia's relatives. The 1871 census records the couple with their ten children living in Poorhouse Yard, now known as Harbour Cottages, behind St. Martins in the High Street. After John Henry was drowned at sea in 1872, a year later, Eliza married her brother-in-law, Jefferson, and had six more children. Jefferson was the innkeeper of The Gloucester in 1885. He too was knocked off his boat *Chance* and drowned when his youngest daughter, Lylie, was only six. Val Gilby, the fourth of Jefferson's six children, orphaned at the age of eleven, went to sea at the age of fourteen in a North Sea trawler operating out of Brightlingsea. He subsequently crewed in Britannia, the racing boat of King George V with two of his brothers, Jim and Edward and in Sir Thomas Lipton's and Sir Thomas Sopwith's yachts. He also formed part of the professional crew of the J-Class yacht Shamrock when it twice competed in the America's Cup. He was joined by his two sons, Jack and Ted. Ted was for

Lady Gifford leading her VADs through Chichester at a victory parade

many years boatman at the Bosham Sailing Club.

Originally from Dorset, John Joseph Strange came to Harts Farm, Bosham, in 1896, with his wife, six sons and four daughters. George, the eldest of the ten, rented and then bought Hoe Farm. The soil of Hoe Farm was not of the best, so George Strange, after marrying Nellie Brown, one of the daughters of the miller, George Brown, in 1926, bought Rectory Farm, from the Cheesmans. Richard Strange, George's grandson and the present farmer, lives in the house next door to Strange Hall, now called Rectory Farm, formerly known as Burnthouse. This farm's tithe barn had become redundant as the jobs of lay rector and collector of tithes had been abolished. The tithe barn was rebuilt in 1932 and the 100,000 tiles from the old one went to re-roof the Royal Observatory at Herstmonceux Castle in East Sussex. George Strange retired in 1947 and his son, Douglas, took over the farm. Douglas, as a teenager, used to help his uncle, George Brown, milk the cows and deliver the milk around the village. Miller Brown's cows used to graze on the fields where now are Critchfield Road, Sunny Way, the Holdens and Marcuse Fields.

John Joseph arranged for all his sons to rent local farms in the area while he himself farmed Mile's Farm, School Lane. In the 1937 Kelly's Directory there were four Strange farmers listed: Frank Strange rented Hart's and Fletcher's Farms which were inherited by John Strange, George at Rectory Farm, Harold at Lees Farm and Joseph Ernest at Mile's Farm, off Taylors Lane This area is now a housing estate the roads of which bear such names as Shamrock, Leander and Westbrook, named after famous yachts crewed by Bosham men. In the mid 1950's, the house formerly known as Rectory House was renamed Strange Hall. A ghost was invented thus adding to the subsequent sale price!

Spectators at a Point to Point held at Old Park

Members of the Strange family also married into other local families while the descendants of John Joseph and Amelia Strange are now the only surviving farming family living in Bosham. (More of the Strange family's farming activities can be found on Page 112).

Although the Brown family had been remotely connected with Bosham for many years, it was not until about the 1870s that John Brown and his wife Mary Ann with their two children leased Bosham Mill and lived in The Mill House, alongside the brook. John died in 1888 and their son George, with his mother, continued to lease the mill; he married Ida Gardner as his first wife and it was their eldest daughter, Nellie, who married George Strange of Harts Farm. George Strange's sister, Gladys, married Frank Follett, owner of the grocer's shop in the High Street. It was George and Ida's son, Charles, who was christened by the vicar, Kenneth MacDermott, in 1903, in the recast church bell before it was re-hung. George Brown's name is engraved on the bell together with John Heaver's, both churchwardens at the time. Charles Brown continued in the milling trade, running a small electric mill in the farm opposite the United Reformed Church in Bosham Lane. In 1953 Margaret Brown, granddaughter of George Brown, married Peter Follett, Frank's son. The Follett family had first come to Bosham in about 1897 when they took over the General Stores in the High Street. Frank Follett sold out to E.J. and L.F. Hines in the late 1920s.

There is no record of any member of the Berkeley family, who had inherited the Lordship of the Manor of Bosham in 1483, living in the village until 1810 when Maurice Frederick, the second illegitimate son of the 5th Earl Berkeley, inherited Bosham. He settled in Old Park, the large house behind the Black Boy Inn at Fishbourne. Maurice rose to the rank of admiral and was created in 1861 Baron Fitzhardinge in recognition of his naval service and parliamentary record. In 1823, Maurice had married Charlotte, a daughter of the 4th Duke of Richmond of Goodwood She died of cholera in 1833, leaving four children. There are memorials to her and to Maurice in Bosham church. A year later he married Lady Charlotte Moreton third daughter of the Earl of Dulcie, but had no children by her. Captain Maurice Berkeley, Royal Navy, in 1834, gave the land for the new National School at the top of School Creek. He also promised an annual subscription of £10 for the upkeep of the school. Charles Paget, second son of Maurice, became the 3rd Baron Fitzhardinge on the death of his father in 1867 and was granted a life interest in Bosham. Although he was childless, he took a tremendous interest in the village, being a church warden for many years. On inheriting Berkeley Castle, he sold the life interest in Bosham to his nephew Edric the 3rd Baron Gifford.

After many years service in the army, where he won a VC in the Zulu war, Edric married, in 1880, a general's daughter, Sophia Street. It was this couple who were to make an impact on

Bosham, being the leading lights of many of the local activities. Lady Gifford was Master of a pack of harrier hounds, which met twice a week until 1915, as well as holding point-to-points in the grounds of Old Park. She took a party of local ladies as VADs (Voluntary Aid Detachment - assistant nurses) to the Boer War in South Africa in 1900 as well as to France during the 1st World War. She contributed financially to many local charities - everyone in Bosham knew it was well worthwhile taking their collecting boxes on the long walk from the centre of the village to Old Park, for Lady Gifford could be counted on to give generously to such things as the Guy Fawkes fireworks parties, the church fêtes, the annual regattas and many other local events.

Edric died in 1911 and is buried in the burial ground, the land which he had given to the church for the purpose; there is also a memorial plaque to him in the church. On his death, Lady Gifford became the Lord of the Manor until 1916, when Edric's brother, Edgar Berkeley Gifford, the 4th Baron, took over the Lordship, Edric and Sophia being childless. Lady Gifford died in 1947. (More of the Berkeley family in Chapters 6 and 12).

The Gatehouse family are remembered for their ownership and management of Broadbridge Mill for over sixty years, details of which can be found elsewhere in this book. They are also remembered on the war memorial on Quay Meadow, where there are inscribed the names of the three sons of John and Marion Gatehouse - John, Thomas and Cuthbert - all three killed in the 1st World War.

There is a story told by Mrs. Eva Purser of an event that she witnessed as a child sometime between 1890 and 1900. Eva was in church one Sunday morning when, during the service, a stranger came in and handed a letter to a young man who was sitting with the Gatehouse family. Mr. & Mrs. Thomas Gatehouse had two daughters, one of whom was very musical and lived in London. She brought down for the weekend a young man whom she hoped to marry, but of whom her father did not approve and who was the recipient of this letter. The service over and as everyone was leaving the church, there was a row of men leaning over the church wall, booing the young lady's male friend. It transpired that the letter read "go back to your wife and children". The young man doffed his hat to the line of men and was never seen again.

Another family that have left their mark in Bosham are the Selwyn Lloyds - (no relations of the politician). Humphrey Selwyn Lloyd, with his wife, Caroline, and Humphrey's Aunt Dora came to Bosham in 1901 when they purchased the Manor House. Here two of their three children were born. 'Hum' as he was known, had had to give up training as a doctor due to ill-health and appears to have spent his time in Bosham organising all manner of things - from church fêtes to photographing the regattas; in short, spending his time doing charitable good works. He laboured hard and long with official

141

BOSHAM BY THE SEA.

Written and Composed by   H. SELWYN LLOYD.

Moderato.

*Humphrey Selwyn Lloyd in the grounds of the Manor House
in the early 1900s*

. cean, There are   won - ders   on___ the   land; ___ There are
. sia,   The   rock - y   coast___ of   Spain, ___ The
. row,   Ours may be   peace___ or   pain; ___ Yet we

bodies getting water mains and main drainage to Bosham. He was an enthusiastic photographer and the photographs that he took of fêtes and regattas, of the Manor House and of all manner of village activities, still survive. In his diaries he recounts how he would take three photos from the same position, but in one there would be the simple landscape, the next one would include one person and the third two people; these photographs were sold at church fêtes for 6d., (2½p), 1/- (5p) and 1/6d (7½p) respectively. There is an envelope dated 9th May, 1911 on the outside of which is an account to Mr.

Lloyd for the printing of six prints at 3d. (1p.) each - a total of 1s.6d (7¹/₂p.).

He with his wife, Caroline, organised, composed and produced many musical shows raising considerable sums of money for charity. He wrote the words for the song "Bosham by the Sea"sung to the tune of the Eton Boating Song, copies of which he also sold at the church fête. He sold the Manor House in 1914 and bought a 14 year lease on The Grange, now the Millstream Hotel. However, a few years later he sub-let The Grange to a hotel proprietor named Germain. This was the beginning of the Millstream Hotel becoming a guesthouse and later a hotel. 'Hum' Lloyd became a British Consul in various places in Europe and the family never lived in Bosham again. All, however, are buried in Bosham burial ground - 'Hum', Caroline, their son Selwyn (who died in 1945 as a result of war service in the Far East) and their daughter, Dorothea. Their third child, John, had died as a child.

Another family that came and went during the 20th century was the Allens. Hugh Allen was appointed Assistant Organist at Chichester Cathedral in 1887. While there he developed a love of sailing and of Chichester Harbour, first having an old potato boat, *Little Florence*, and then buying the yacht *Buttercup*. In 1919, he and his wife, Winifred, purchased for £1,300 the western half of what is now known as Bosham Hoe from Frederick Sadler, the Chichester corn merchant. Here they built two houses, Furzefield and Furzefield Cottage, on the ruins of the brickmakers cottages which had stood there. While the building went on, the family lived in a barge tied up alongside Furzefield Jetty, one which had been used for decades for the boats bringing the workmen over from Itchenor to the brick building works, there being no road access from Bosham. The brickyard ceased operating in 1919.

In 1923 Lady Allen was to purchase the rest of the Hoe for £1,250, but within seven years she had sold most of her original purchase of the Furzefield houses and land which, in 1946, she was to re-purchase. In the 1930s it had been her plan to form a small hamlet with a marina on Lighters' Field on the Hoe, for there was deep water anchorage at all stages of the tide off Tuffs Hard. The deeds of the then six Tuffs Hard houses, built in 1937, show plans for a clubhouse, a ships' chandlery, a grocer's shop and six lock-up garages or boathouses. The war intervened and in 1946 planning permission was refused for any further development on Tuffs Hard, on the grounds that there were already too many houses to the rural acre in this area! This decision was to be reversed only a few years later. By 1936 Lady Allen had built a number of houses on the Hoe, one for herself and smaller ones which she let only to young married naval officers. So the 1950s saw many young wives pushing prams around the Hoe, while there were no less than two kindergartens at various times on the estate. Also at this time, Lady Allen commenced selling off single plots of land for private residential development, till by 1957 there were no less than thirty-seven houses on the estate - one of which was Lady Allen's own house called The Hoe. By then Lady Allen was approaching eighty; her husband had died in 1946, and she wished to dispense with the pressures of running an estate. She therefore set in motion the necessary work for the residents to form themselves into a company. Thus was formed the Hoe Estate Co. Ltd. Lady Allen died in 1966, her only son, Sir Richard Allen, a former Ambassador to Burma, died in 1996 aged 95, while his son, David, had been killed in a car accident in 1982. The gates to the Church Path were given by Lady Allen in memory of her husband, Sir Hugh Allen. Her only surviving granddaughter no longer owns any property on the estate. Today there are some fifty seven houses on the Hoe

Gerald Marcuse's fire engine in 1947, garaged opposite the Congregational church in Bosham Lane

Estate Co. Ltd. a company managed by the residents themselves. Lady Allen had the gates at the entrance to Church Path made by the blacksmith Norman Redman in memory of her husband Hugh.

Gerald Marcuse, born in 1884, a pioneer of Empire Broadcasting, was another character who, while only living in Bosham for a few years, nevertheless left his mark on the village. He is honoured by a seat placed by the brook on Quay Meadow, after his death in 1961, by the Old Timers' Association of the Radio Society of Great Britain. By profession an engineer, he travelled all over the world, including Russia. It was during his travels that he began his pioneer work in radio, particularly in various parts of the British Empire, beginning operations in 1913. From 1924 he was making radio contact with ships in the Arctic, the US Fleet sailing between Honolulu and Australia and with the Naval Base in Hong Kong. In 1925 he began broadcasting concerts to US amateurs from the Savoy Hotel in London. In 1925 his call sign G2NM was picked up in Japan and in 1927 he was granted an Empire licence. Subsequently he became Chairman of the International Amateur Radio Union. During the 2nd World War he did secret work for the government – it was then that he moved to Tidewaters, Windmill Fields, Bosham, where a position on the coast was obviously necessary for his work. Later when Windmill Fields were being developed, one of the roads, Marcuse Fields, was named after him.

Distressed when a house in Bosham

was burned to the ground for lack of a local fire engine, Marcuse bought in 1947 a redundant fire engine from Chichester and formed the Bosham Volunteer Fire Brigade. He also obtained from Farmer Brown of the Mill the loan of a barn opposite the United Reformed Church in Bosham Lane in which to garage the vehicle. He ran the brigade for ten years until the station moved to Critchfield Road. Later the management of the Bosham station was taken over by the Chichester fire station, some of the early volunteers included members of the Strange and Arnold families. Marcuse was also a County Councillor from 1950-54. His name lives on, for his widow, Irene, gave all his equipment to the Working Museum at Amberley, West Sussex.

Donald Turnbull, the son of a former Mayor of Chichester, brought his family to Bosham after the 2nd World War. Donald purchased some land from the church and started Oakcroft Nurseries in Walton Lane in 1946. The land had been part of the garden of the former Vicarage, now called Walton House, where in the early years of the 20th century, the church fêtes were held and which later had been used as allotments. Donald, a territorial soldier, had spent the war years in the Army but on demobilisation, he re-erected in the Vicarage garden, a greenhouse and shed that he had had elsewhere, as well as building himself a house. The nurseries initially grew fruit, later changing to flowers and then salad crops. Donald's son, Michael, after leaving the Merchant Navy in 1956, joined his father, who gave his newly married son a plot in a corner of the field on which they too built a bungalow. Michael's wife, Iris, soon became a leading light in various

Oakcroft Nurseries in Walton Lane

145

activities in Bosham, which included two spells as President of Bosham Women's Institute. She also started the Bosham Flower Club, which is now a thriving group in the village, as well as forming and conducting a Women's Institute singing group, afterwards to become the Bosham Singers. Oakcroft Nurseries became a flourishing business, diversifying to develop a pick-your-own soft fruit venture. Donald died in 1961 and Michael and his young family then moved into his parents home, while his widowed mother lived in a caravan in the garden. He was later to be joined by his son, Philip. In March 1996, the Turnbulls celebrated fifty years of nursery gardening with two acres of greenhouses. Unfortunately, problems arose, the nursery had to be sold, Philip joined the fire service, while Michael and Iris moved to Emsworth. Iris died in 2003.

One of the great characters in Bosham for many years was 'Speedo' Paine, a name he acquired by the fact that he was always rushing everywhere. Although born in Chichester in 1902 he married a Bosham girl, Jessie Gristwood whose parents lived in Green Acre, School Lane. Later Speedo and Jessie were to move into Green Acre to look after her old parents, where he had a wonderful vegetable garden and bred pigs. He also became a specialist in growing sweet peas. Speedo had many jobs in the area, one of his last was helping out at the Bosham Sailing Club. Speedo was always to be seen bicycling around the village with his faithful dog, Gus, a half-whippet, half -greyhound bitch, at his heel. In his old age, Speedo was given a small Instamatic camera and thereafter was always photographing, with slide films, the sunrises and sunsets; these were shown to many local organisations, particularly the Monday Club, the over 60s club in the village, although Speedo himself hardly bothered to look at them. He would get up at all hours of the morning to take such sunrises. He was also a regular visitor to The Anchor where he had his favourite perch from which he could see everybody entering the hostelry - heaven help any unsuspecting person who should dare to occupy that seat. When he died, a memorial plaque was inserted into the wall of his favourite lookout position - "Speedo 2.11.79"

The internationally famous American dramatist and poet, T.S. Eliot, spent many of the summer months staying in Bosham, first with his wife Vivien and after her death with his second wife, Valerie. Nearly every year from 1916 onwards they took rooms at a house on the Trippet, the coastal path formerly called the Craut or High Path. South View, a house now called Mariners, was owned by Miss Kate Smith, described as a kindly soul and a good cook. In addition to running this small 'pension', she cared for her severely disabled brother-in-law, James Tullett. Vivien Eliot, it would appear, was a highly strung neurotic woman and Tom Eliot felt that the sea air and quiet atmosphere of Bosham would have a beneficial effect on his ever-ailing first wife. Tom wrote of the village 'the

An artist at work by the church gates in the High Street

natives are charming, like New England country people, both in aspect and accent. They use 'sir' rather more, but are equally keen on making money out of visitors'. Year after year, the Eliots sailed, visited friends often by water, walked on the Downs and drank in The Anchor. It was always a sad moment when, summer over, it was time to return to their London home.

The beauty of Bosham has drawn artists from all over the world for many generations, arriving by carriage, horse, boat, train and, more recently by motor car. One of the earliest must be Grimm, a Sussex painter whose works are now in the British Library. Those of Bosham were sketched around 1782, the most famous being of the church, the Mill House and the college; this includes the sight of a mast behind the buildings. He also painted one of the college buildings, a survival from those occupied by the Austin Canons over many centuries, situated immediately opposite the church. There are also sketches he made of the corbels (stone figureheads) used to hold up the rafters of the chancel roof some of which are still visible. Many of his paintings were made into etchings (see Page 27).

There are accounts of how parties of artists regularly came over from a Paris art school in the late 1800s. Arriving in Bosham by train, they were transported by waggonette down to the centre of the village to stay in one of the guest houses there. To quote from the words of one artist – 'scattered everywhere are the artists. Ladies in shapeless pinafores and large white sun-bonnets sketching, everywhere artists painting the water and the boats and the wrecks'.

There are many drawings and paintings by R.H. Nibbs, from which etchings were made. One painting of

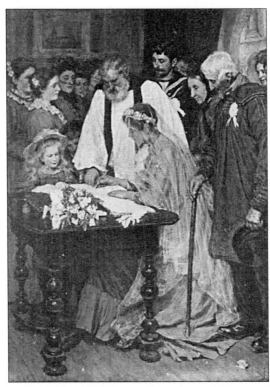

James Charles' painting of a mock signing of the parish register, which was exhibited at the Royal Academy in 1895. Alfred Hickman took the part of the clergyman; the bride was Annie Curtis & the groom Henry Moore. The small bridesmaid was the artist's daughter & behind her (face half hidden) stood Maggie Stoveld. Witnesses included Joseph Major, Granny Apps & Mrs Treagus

the mid-19th century is of the familiar view of the church, quay and the Downs in the background which was sold for about £7,500 in 1987. This price was similar to that fetched by another of his paintings 'Bosham - An Early Morning on the Coast' which captured the atmosphere of Bosham so well. The very famous marine artist, Charles William Wyllie included Bosham in his repertoire with a painting, exhibited at the Royal Academy in 1888 called 'All on a Summer's Day at Bosham, Sussex'.

Few of the artists who have left paintings of Bosham, lived in the village. One notable exception was Henry Henshall (1856-1928) who lived on Gosportside and who did the illustrations for the vicar, Kenneth MacDermott's, book 'Bosham Church: Its History and Antiquities'. Henry exhibited many pictures at the Royal Academy and was also a Member of the Royal Society of Painters in watercolours (RWS) Many of his paintings are of local people of the time. Another artist who lived at Lower Hone Farm was

Henry Herbert La Thangue, RA (1859-1929) who painted many of the local characters. His painting 'The Man with a Scythe' depicts three Bosham girls, Trixie Balchin (neé Apps), Pauline Harmer (neé Collins) and Mrs. Tukes. Thangue's great friend was James Charles, who lived at Colner House at the western end of the village and was also famous for his paintings of the locals, which included one of a mock wedding held in the vestry, using local characters for the tableaux. Another painting of 1888 entitled 'Children Paddling' shows the windmill, now remembered in the area known as Windmill Fields. Another painter, Eileen Robey, the daughter of the well known comedian, George Robey, lived for many years in Rose Cottage, next door to The Berkeley Arms. It always seemed to the locals that she spent more time in the 'Berks' than she did in her own home. Eileen Robey's brother, Mr. Justice Robey, was a distinguished judge.

Many of these paintings were to find their way into some of the lesser art galleries around Britain. In spite of Bosham being a Mecca for artists it is surprising how few are to be found for sale in local galleries or antique shops.

'Words of Comfort' by Henry Henshall, who did the illustrations for Kenneth MacDermott's book Bosham, it's History & Antiquities. *Eli Matthews was the old man & Mrs. Harding the old lady, painted in a cottage living room*

There are many more families who deserve a mention in this chapter, but it is impossible to include them all, if for no other reason than that details of their lives cannot be found. It is sad that so many of the families that have lived in Bosham for many generations have now dispersed all over the world in just a few decades. However, air travel and easy communications frequently see them visit their roots, to look up their family trees in the local Record Office, write their names in the church visitors' book and walk the roads of Bosham looking for their old family homes.

The Waterfront

CHAPTER 12

From Cottages to Manors

It is difficult to identify the oldest house in the village, for owners are usually so proud of their properties that they struggle madly to prove that theirs must be The One. The first permanent settlements in the Bosham area would have been groups of one-roomed, round houses made of wattle and daub with thatched roofs such as one still sees in Africa today. The original inhabitants would have been mostly fishermen living along the shore and keeping their small boats alongside their cottages above the high tide level. It is the Romans we have to thank for the concept of separate rooms within one building, each used for a different function such as cooking, sleeping or working. Gradually simply-made dwellings were built alongside the pathways around the village while the materials used became more sophisticated. Timber and flint, found locally, were two plentiful materials used, while more affluent house owners imported stone from such places as Dorset, the Isle of Wight and Caen in France; the same stone that was used in the church. Many of the 17th, 18th and 19th century houses which stand on either side of Bosham Lane today almost certainly started as one-storey timber-framed wattle and daub buildings with thatched roofs. Then, as the art of brickmaking was re-established and as brickworks opened up in the 16th and 17th centuries using the plentiful local clay, wattle was progressively replaced by bricks. The majority of the three and four hundred year old houses in Bosham Lane are now Grade II and III listed buildings, most within the Bosham Conservation Area. Not many have an interesting history, but where there is a

Commander Frederick Jarrad who was Managing Director of the Bosham Dredgerman's Co-operative Society
Photo by courtesy of Mark Jarrad

story to be told, it is given below.

One can usually expect the 'Big House' in a village such as Bosham to be The Manor House and occupied by the Lord of the Manor. There is little evidence that any Lord of the Manor occupied what is now called The Manor House during the last six hundred years, although maps of 1784 and 1821 show the building in the ownership of the Berkeley family, who were successively Lords of the Manor. This large house next door to the church was used as a farmhouse for decades, if not centuries, and called Manor Farm. It was Commander Frederick Jarrad, Royal Navy, who bought the farmhouse sometime prior to 1859 and renamed it The Manor House. In 1894 it was recorded that F.W. Jarrad was the Managing Director of the Bosham Dredgermen's Co-operative Society Ltd. Between 1881 and 1885, four children of Frederick and Sara Jarrad were christened in Bosham church while the family are listed in the 1891 and 1901 census returns. In 1901 the property was sold to Humphrey Selwyn Lloyd.

The dining room is the oldest part of the house which dates back to 1350. Under a stone in the centre of the room there are steps which may have led to underground passages leading to the church and The Anchor pub. Halfway up the main staircase, there is an attic room which could have been part of a tower – viewed from the outside, it certainly looks like one. The major part of the house is of the 17th century but Roman bricks as well as Caen stone similar to those in the church, have been used in the construction of some of the outside walls. It has been suggested that the house was built on the site of Canute's mansion, which later may have formed

A sketch of the Manor House in 1978

152

part of King Harold's moated palace. There are the remains of Saxon walls, with windows and a doorway alongside the brook on the west side of the grounds of the present house. There are also waterways on the north and east sides of the house which would have formed part of the moat. Paintings by Grimm of 1782 show a watercourse on the south side of these grounds adjacent to the church, indicating that the curtilage was completely surrounded by water at some time.

Like many old houses, The Manor House had its ghosts. Selwyn Lloyd, who lived in it until 1919, records in his diaries the story of an old woman who was frequently seen up to the 1914-18 war, sitting spinning in the dining room. There was another of an old man dressed in brown who appeared in the oak room, the north attic over the drawing room. There was also the ghost of Edward Bennett who was frequently seen by the Lloyds as well as by previous owners of the house, sitting in a chair in the main bedroom facing out to sea. The story goes that Edward quarrelled with one of his sons, who went off to sea, never to return. During his last illness, Edward sat in the window, praying that his son would return – he died, a broken hearted man, his wish unfulfilled.

Above: The room with a window jutting out from the roof in the centre of the picture may have originally formed part of a tower and be the oldest part of the building

Right: The Gardener sisters, house maids at the Manor house in 1901. One of Humphrey Selwyn Lloyd's photographs

Although for one hundred and fifty years the Bennett family owned a considerable part of Bosham, they must have been tenants of the Lord of the Manor who is recorded in documents of the time as the owner. An Edward Bennett was churchwarden at Bosham Church in 1743, 1750 and 1786. In 1779 an Edward Bennett was Chamberlain of the Manor of Bosham as well as town clerk of Chichester. (As almost every eldest son of the Bennett family was named Edward, it is difficult to know to which one the records refer). Selwyn Lloyd found in the grounds of The Manor round glass medallions of the type found on the sides of wine bottles marked 'Edward Bennett 1760'. It is believed that the present front hall was used as a brewhouse at some time.

While they lived in the Manor, the Lloyds engaged an expert to look at some of the massive black oak beams; it was the expert's opinion that the beams were at least six hundred years old and were good for at least another three hundred.

Old Park, a Grade II listed house, is at the extreme eastern end of the old parish boundaries. It dates back to at least the 17th century – within the present building there is a small timber framed building which could have formed part of a three-bay hall house. There is a date, 1713, over one of the windows but this probably refers to the date when new windows were installed; a hundred years later the walls of the building were re-faced. There were further additions in the 18th, 19th and 20th centuries. In the Manor of Bosham Rental Book it is recorded that in 1768 an Edward Bennett rented 'Old Parke'.

Maurice Frederick Fitzhardinge inherited the Manor of Bosham from his father, 5th Earl Berkeley, in 1810 and is thought to have taken up residence in Old Park After his marriage in 1823, to Charlotte, daughter of Charles, 4th Duke of Richmond, they did make their home in Old Park but Maurice probably spent little time here owing to his naval duties. In 1867 Maurice's son, Charles Paget, inherited the Manor and, it is thought, he too lived in Old Park, although in the 1881 census Samuel Davenport, an accountant, with his wife, two young children and nine servants, are recorded as occupying the house. In 1897, the childless Charles Paget inherited Berkeley Castle and, two years later, sold the life interest of the Manor of Bosham for £7,500 to his nephew, Edric Frederick Gifford, 3rd Baron Gifford. Edric was the elder son of Charles's sister, Lady Frederica Charlotte, who in 1845 had married Robert Gifford, the 2nd Baron. The 3rd Baron, with his wife, the former Sophia Street lived in Old Park and entered fully into all the activities of the village. The Giffords continued to live in Old Park until 1919 when the fourth Baron and Lord of the Manor, sold the Lordship which included Old Park, to Albert Eadie.

Albert Eadie occupied the house for the six years that he held the Lordship. No Lord of the Manor has lived in Old Park since. From 1810 to 1919 the Berkeley Lords of the Manor were, in theory at least, resident in

WEST SUSSEX.

BOSHAM near CHICHESTER.

Bounded by the Bosham and Chichester Channels; close to Bosham Station; two miles from the busy Markets of Chichester.

Particulars, Plan, Views and Conditions of Sale

OF

The Valuable Freehold Agricultural, Residential and Sporting Properties

KNOWN AS

THE BOSHAM ESTATE

In the Old Manor of Bosham

COMPRISING SOME OF THE RICHEST CORN & GRASS LANDS IN ENGLAND

INCLUDING

"OLD PARK"

A GENTLEMAN'S RESIDENCE, with Hall, Four Reception Rooms, Twelve Bed Rooms, Two Bath Rooms, etc.   Stabling, Garages, Pretty Grounds, Large Fruit and Vegetable Gardens and Rich Park Pastures about 25 ACRES.

A First-class Agricultural and Sporting Estate of about 778 Acres

Including OLD PARK FARM or Home Farm, with Excellent Farmhouse and Eight Modern Cottages (440 Acres WITH POSSESSION), also

CHURCH and HOOK FARM of about 202 ACRES, with excellent Farmhouse and Five good Cottages, and

128 ACRES OF WOODLANDS providing MOST EXCELLENT and WELL-PRESERVED SHOOTING offering continuous good sport. Small Shooting Lodge.

SOUTHWOOD FARM, 365 Acres, WITH POSSESSION

A Rich Corn and Stock Holding, with very good House and Buildings and Six Cottages, and VALUABLE BUILDING FRONTAGE to BOSHAM CHANNEL facing the Ancient Village of Bosham.

LOWERHONE FARM, 132 Acres

With Capital Farmhouse and Four Cottages.

SMALL HOLDINGS, BUILDING and ACCOMMODATION LANDS

and the OLD SCHOOL HOUSE, Bosham, and Two Acres on Bosham Channel, WITH UNIQUE YACHTING, FISHING AND WILD FOWL SHOOTING FACILITIES.

The whole extending to about

1,442 Acres.

HAMPTON & SONS
in conjunction with Messrs.
STRIDE & SON

Will Sell the above by Auction,

AT THE DOLPHIN HOTEL, CHICHESTER,

On **WEDNESDAY, the 27th day of SEPTEMBER, 1922,**

At 2.30 o'clock precisely, IN EIGHT LOTS (unless previously sold privately).

VENDOR'S SOLICITORS—Messrs. FRANCIS & CROOKENDEN,
23, Lincoln's Inn Fields, W.C. 2.

Particulars, with Plan, Views and Conditions of Sale may be obtained of Messrs. STRIDE & SON,

Bosham – could Old Park be considered the manor house of Bosham for those one hundred and nine years? This building was named as a manor house in 1557 but of which village? Old Fishbourne was part of the Manor and Parish of Bosham until 1988 when Fishbourne formed its own parish council, incorporating the two Fishbournes, Old and New, so Old Park is now in the Parish of Fishbourne. Today Old Park stands on the edge of Fishbourne Creek, an imposing 18th century mansion with many outbuildings, occupied by a young family who are busy refurbishing the house.

About two miles south of Old Park is Old Park Farm House, a 16th century timber built yeoman's' farmhouse also, for many centuries, part of the Manor of Bosham and owned by the Berkeleys. The 1746 Manor of Bosham Rental Book records that Thomas Pope leased Park Farm for twenty one years at the annual rent of £115 'plus an annual gift at Christmas of two couples of capons or alternatively five shillings' (25p.). John Peskett leased the house until at least 1875. This was one of the properties sold by the Berkeleys in 1919.

The Old Park woods are now the only woodlands left in Bosham. A map of the 18th century shows a much larger area of woodland than there is now which then covered most of the southern half of the Bosham peninsula. These woods are first mentioned in the Close Rolls of 1233.

A short distance from Old Park Farm House is Field House. One and three quarter miles east of Bosham church, Field House, formerly called Church Farm House, is a 16th century Grade II listed timber-framed building with the exterior walls built of brick. On a map of 1778, it was called Hook Farm but in the Land Tax Assessment of 1780-1832 the house was named 'Church Farm, Old Park Lane'. For a building to have the name Church Farm House, one of three so named in Bosham, it must have been given to and owned by the Church at some time.

Internal examination shows the original yeoman's farmhouse with a large central chimney and two fireplaces, with a third upstairs, where there is also Elizabethan wooden panelling. In the 16th century the hall house concept had been abandoned to be replaced by rooms built at each end of an upper floor of the hall and the whole heated by a massive central fireplace with a chimney. The fireplace downstairs has an inglenook with a bread oven, as well as holes which would have supported a spit. In 1784, the house was owned and occupied by William Smith, a woolcomber, (a person who combs or cards wool); the land comprised thirteen fields, the rest of the surrounding land being owned by the Berkeleys. In 1761 a William Smith owned Hook and Walton Farms too and, by 1785, he also owned a mill with house and land. It is not recorded which mill. His father had died a wealthy man in 1759 leaving over £1,546 to his widow. Also in 1759, a William Smith was Constable of the Manor of Bosham, but he did not hold this office for long for he died in 1762. In 1791, an Edward Bennett bought Church Farm but he lived in the house for only two years, selling it in 1831; again it is difficult to know which Edward Bennett. Many of the old farm buildings and barns of Church Farm have been converted into separate dwellings and retain the name 'Church Farm, Old Park Lane'.

Past Field House, down Hook Lane, is Hook Farm, a Tudor building which owned its own oyster beds. The walls of the farmhouse

ships which arrived from the Mediterranean to load up with the local corn at Fishbourne.

Another of the farms which had been part of the Manor of Bosham and only a short distance from Church Farm, Old Park Lane, was Hoe Farm. Although the main part of this farmhouse was built in 1740, there are parts which are considerably older. Situated on the southern end of the Bosham peninsula, the farmlands consisted of almost all the area now known as The Hoe, Fletcher's Fields, (bounded by Fletcher's Lane) all the fields in the eastern portion of what is

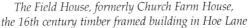

*The Field House, formerly Church Farm House,
the 16th century timber framed building in Hoe Lane*

include stones from Ostia, a city in Italy at the mouth of the Tiber. These stones must have come as ballast, for the only cargo imported here at that time would have been of spices, a very light commodity; something heavier would have been required in the holds of the

now known as Smuggler's Lane, (formerly Penzance Lane), as well as a part of Hart's Farm, a total of over one hundred and seventy nine acres. In 1923, Frederick Sadler, the grain merchant of Chichester, sold Hoe Farm and fifty eight acres to George Strange, who had already been renting this farm for some years. Within three years George had sold it and moved to Rectory Farm in Walton Lane. There is an inscription on the former cattle sheds of Hoe Farm 'G.H. Weston June 1807'. Further round the Bosham peninsula is Lower Hone Farm, the main part of which was built in 1775.

In the London *Times* of Friday, August 9th 1867, there is a notice of an auction to be held, when three lots of freehold and copyhold estates were to

1. Old Park in 2005

2. Old Park Farmhouse, Old Park Lane in 1995

Hoe Farm after a major renovation in 2000

be sold containing 347 statute acres, comprising Lower Hone, Hart's and Fletcher's Farms with farmhouses, buildings and labourers' cottages 'the whole let to respectable and responsible tenants....... the whole producing an annual rental of above £700 per annum'. This would have been a sizeable income for a purchaser of these three estates.

Past Lower Hone Farm, along Shore Road, is The Red House, built in the late 1930s in the days of cooks, maids and housekeepers. It had accommodation for staff on the top floor, no central heating but open fires in most of the rooms. It was the first of many houses which, after the war, would be built along Shore Road at the end of the row of shore-side cottages which formed Gosportside. Gosportside (meaning opposite the port – Bosham Quay being the port) had been a hamlet on its own and had had its own pub and shop. The 2nd World War came before the owners had a chance to occupy the completed Red House, for in 1939 it was commandeered for use by the Royal Marines, though later members of the Women's Land Army occupied it. There was a large kitchen garden which was registered as a smallholding, enabling the family to have poultry and a paid gardener to look after it. The house was a wreck when it was de-requisitioned at the end of the war. In restoring the house, the only paint available for its restoration was grey – so grey it was painted. It was later sold and occupied by teachers from Wispers Girls' School at Haslemere in Surrey, and renamed

Wispers Minor. It is thought to have been used as a convalescent home for pupils of the school as well as being occupied by some of the staff. It was later bought by Marianne and Michael Bates, one of the conditions of the sale being that the name of the house be changed, so the Bates renamed the house Silvermere. The present owners have reverted to the original name of The Red House.

Another Tudor hall house was Strange Hall, formerly called Rectory Farm. For nearly one hundred years, the Cheesman family, who were the lay rectors of Bosham, collected the tithes in the nearby barn until, in 1927, the executors of Alfred Cheesman, sold Rectory Farm, together with one hundred and twenty three acres and a number of buildings which included Parkers Pound, to George Strange. In 1958 it was divided into two houses. Parkers Pound was originally two mediaeval timber framed open hall cottages about five feet apart, the first one built in about 1350 with one downstairs room and a centre fireplace. This was at the time of the Black Death so people would have chosen to build new houses outside the village where there was less likelihood of infection. The second cottage was built about one hundred years later. The original occupants were bordars, a status only one above a slave; in short a small farmer who was allowed to occupy a few acres, usually about thirty, but in return had to do jobs for the lord of the manor. The wattle and daub walls of the cottages were later replaced with bricks while the present fireplaces are of the latter half of the 17th century. At one time the buildings were known as Sparke's Cottages and one of them may have been used as an alehouse. During the Depression of 1930, the Stranges were forced to sell the cottages for £500 and this price was to include providing the new owners with straw for thatching. The two cottages were later made into one house and named Parkers Pound. During the 2nd World War the house was used by the RAF.

A few doors away from Parkers Pound is the thatched Laurel Cottage. Built in 1697, thus one of the older houses in the village, it too was owned successively by the Cheesman and Strange families. The Redmans, who were the local blacksmiths for at least one hundred and fifty years until 1982, occupied the house with the forge alongside, the latter now pulled down. The church records show that George Redman, son of the blacksmith, Stephen Redman, was baptised in Bosham in 1839.

Two of the oldest houses in the village are The Old Thatch in Station Road and Broadstream Cottage, the 500 year old Grade II listed thatched cottage on the old main road, now the A259. The Old Thatch, now 450 years old, is a Grade 11 listed house, similar to Pendean Farm house at the Open Air Weald and Downland Museum at Singleton. In 1908 its owner, John Henry Yoxall, was a rigger in the Royal Yacht, The Victoria and Albert.

Broadstream Cottage, is very similar to the reconstructed mediaeval Hangleton Cottage at the open air Weald and Downland Museum and believed to date back to 1460. The original walls were made of clay and sea heather – there was no wood used in its original construction, for the wooden timbers were added later. The thatch for the roof was laid directly on to pine poles, believed to have come from Norway. Coins found in the building included a number from the reign of Antonurius (there is no record of who he might have been, possibly a local

Parkers Pound, formerly two 14th century timber framed open hall cottages

PARKERS POUND

1. Strange Hall north

2 Strange Hall south formerly Rectory Farm

3. Laurel cottage in Walton Lane, occupied by the Redman family who were blacksmiths in the village for a hundred and fifty years. The forge can be seen on the left

4. Dave & Irene Stunt stand at the gate of Broadstream Cottage on the old main road, now Old Bridge Road. Here, many years ago, the honey-woman put out her home grown vegetables and honey for sale

Roman governor). Thus it would appear that there must have been some form of occupation here during Roman times; the cottage would have been near the old Roman road from Chichester to Southampton. Known as Pound Cottage, Tollgate Road, in 1880 it was owned by Frederick Fitzhardinge Maurice Berkeley and leased to John Pescott, probably of the same family as John Peskett who rented Old Park in the 1870s. (The spelling of names was how the scribe of the time chose to interpret the words as spoken to him, for few people would have been able to write their own names.) Just across the road from Pound Cottage was the village pound, where loose cattle were impounded until the owners paid a fine to reclaim their animals. In the 1890s, a young lady lived in Pound Cottage with her small daughter, the former allegedly thought to be the lady friend of the defrocked vicar who lived in Critchfield House, while the little girl was thought to be their daughter. There was no evidence to support this allegation, but nevertheless the poor woman was ostracised by most of the village.

Broadstream Cottage later came into the ownership of a bee specialist, Mrs Clark when the house was known locally as the Honeywoman's Cottage. Mrs. Clark used to sell her home produced products of honey, apples, plums, eggs, tomatoes and rhubarb, when in season, from a table outside her garden gate on the edge of the old Turnpike Road. This

The 18th century brick fronted Brook House on Quay Meadow, one of the houses owned at one time by the 2nd Lord Iveagh

162

road is now a cul-de-sac off the A259 and renamed Old Bridge Road.

One would have thought that the oldest houses in the village would be around the church and the High Street – they probably were but have either been knocked down and rebuilt or else 'modernised' with bricks covering the old wattle and daub walls. The answer will never be known until such time as a house needs to be rebuilt or severely altered. During the 17th and 18th centuries, Bosham must have been a prosperous place for there are many brick built largish houses around the village.

One of them, the brick-fronted Brook House, which faces Quay Meadow, was built between 1760 and 1780 on what was probably part of the remains of the curtilage of the old monastery. Included in the garden walls

of this house and visible when walking up the High Street, is a doorway to the old monastery believed to be from the 18th century. Within what is now the garden of Brook House, was the Parsonage House, adapted from the monastery buildings and occupied by the vicar of the parish until 1840, when it was demolished. A dig in 2004 carried out by the Chichester and District Archaeological Society found evidence of mediaeval walls, which had been robbed and replaced by rubble of a later date. This suggested that the original good quality stone of these walls had been of an earlier period and used later for new buildings. Either Brook House or the Mill House was used temporarily as a vicarage before a new one was built at the top of Walton Lane, now Walton House, a surprisingly long way from the church. The Rev. Henry Mitchell was

The 18th century doorway which was probably part of the original monastery.
The other side of this gateway is pictured on page 27

the first vicar to occupy the new house which was completed in 1845. In 1839, the tenement and small garden of the old Parsonage House were sold by auction to Henry Booker for £65. On the outside of the north wall of the garden of Brook House is a tablet built into the wall and inscribed 'L R & M 1743'. There is another similar tablet inset on the inside of the garden wall dated 1763. The initials and dates probably refer to Richard Lawson and his wife Mary who would have lived in the Parsonage House. He was vicar from 1731 to 1771 and had no less than twelve children christened in the church between 1737 and 1759. On the Ordnance Survey map of 1876, this area is given as being 1.942 acres consisting of houses, yards, gardens &c. Brook House was included

in the properties that the 2nd Lord Iveagh purchased when he became Lord of the Manor in 1925. It has since been sold and is no longer owned by the Manor of Bosham Ltd.

The Mill House, which lies adjacent to the brook, was for many years occupied by the miller of the Quay mill, George Brown and his family. George grazed his cows on the surrounding meadows, selling his farm products of milk, cream, butter and eggs from a doorway of the 16th century north section of the house which is on the edge of the brook. Most of the remainder of the house is 17th century while a 19th century addition on the west side (which is seen in many of the old photographs of this house) was pulled down in the 1960s. In 1976, it

The Mill and Quay Cottage

164

was sold by Lady Brigid Ness, daughter of the 2nd Lord Iveagh, one time Lord of the Manor, to Peter Stevens, the owner of the Millstream Hotel at the time. During alterations to the house, the remains of a 10th century stone structure were found under the floor, which suggested that the house had been used, centuries ago, for the manufacture of iron implements. Under the kitchen floor were also found many centuries-old artefacts, including a Roman gaming marble. There was a mediaeval boundary wall on the south side of the garden which had been made of medieval oyster shells, but that too has disappeared.

The building on the edge of the Quay was at one time a double mill with a cottage attached to the north western end. This mill must have been one of those referred to in the Domesday Book of 1086. Rebuilt by the

Right: The side entrance of the Mill House on the edge of the brook, from whence milk, butter and eggs were sold at the kitchen door

Below: The Mill House with Mrs George Brown and her daughter Ruby. The Victorian addition on the left has since been demolished

Lord of the Manor, using as many of the old timbers and tiles as possible, the Bosham Sailing Club took over the building as their clubhouse on 31st March 1956. Although it has few architectural features, the mill is pictorially pleasing, sited as it is on the Quay on the sea approach to the village. This description could also include the thatched Quay Cottage which was originally two cottages, most of it dating back to the 18th century. In 1920, the Bloomfields, the occupiers of Quay Cottage, renovated the interior of the building, making the two cottages into one house.

Further round the shore is a row of cottages now known as Harbour Cottages, formerly called the Poor Houses. It was in this area that the Austin Canons had their cells and college buildings. In 1799 Harbour Cottages were used as a malthouse, then later became the Poor Houses - it is not known how or by whom they were administered for this purpose – and were later occupied by local fishermen. In the 1970s the marble slabs on which the newly caught fish were placed could still be seen in the sculleries of some of the houses.

Backing on to Harbour Cottages is St. Martin's, built in 1734 as two houses and which still have the original separate front doors, while an internal door connects the two dwellings. The house was leased to John Martin by the owner, William Combes, in about 1829. By 1851, according to the census, a dozen members of the Martin family were living there. The house was named as Martin's House in the 1871 census. In 1841, a third son, George, was born to John Martin and his wife Patience. It was this George Martin who, in 1872, eloped with Charlotte Sophia, daughter

St. Martins, the 18th century three storied house built as two houses with two front doors side by side

of the incumbent, Mr. Mitchell. In a village renowned for nicknames for everything and everybody, it may be that Martin's acquired the addition of 'Saint' to its name when George married into the church, so to speak. John purchased the entire building in 1869; one of his daughters, Mary Anne, lived with her husband, Harry Aldous, and their family in one half. John died in 1882 and his widow, Patience, lived in the other half until her death in 1894. Patience's half was sold to Mary Ann Brown, mother of the miller, George Brown. Since then there have been a series of owners, who have all maintained the building extremely well; thus a good number of the original features still remain. Over the years, the only alterations appear to be to the kitchen area, so the house remains an excellent example of a well-built Georgian house, albeit always divided into two dwellings.

Next door to St. Martin's is the 300 year old Galleon House, a Grade II listed Queen Anne house. It had been called Bay Tree House and was at one time a grocer's shop owned by members of the Martin family; relatives of this family also ran the two inns in the High Street, The Ship and The Anchor. It then became the village sweet shop run by Mrs. Annie Stoveld who purchased the property in 1917 from funds raised to help the widows of Bosham seamen who had been drowned at about that time. There remains the mid-nineteenth century shop window, on which there is a preservation order.

Mrs. Stoveld had a tinkling bell on the door of her shop to warn her of the arrival of a customer. Some of the older people in the village recall that, as children, they would tease Mrs. Stoveld by running in and out of the shop to activate the bell, so calling her out needlessly.

Galleon House has been called by many names. Mabel Stoveld, the last surviving child of Annie who had died in 1964, made a flat for herself in part of the old sweet shop, retaining the name Bay Tree House. But the house must have been divided before that, for the northern half was known as Bychurch and occupied in 1939 by Mr. and Mrs. Gregory Major, the parents of Annie Stoveld. At the beginning of the war, the Majors had taken in an evacuee, Albert Robertson, from Wimbledon in London. During her visit to Bosham on December 9th 1939, Queen Elizabeth, consort of King George VI, called on the Majors to meet young Albert and stayed for a cup of tea. Mabel Stoveld died in 1991 and the house is back to being one establishment, now called Galleon House.

Probably the first of the many serious weekenders to Bosham was the Ogilvie family. Heneage Ogilvie was a London surgeon, who with his wife, Magdalen, first visited Bosham in 1925 and fell in love with the little village. They were able to rent a small cottage for £1.10s a week (£1.50p), one of a row of fishermen's cottages in the High Street called Bosham Castle. There was no indoor sanitation; only a hole in the floor in the room on the sea side, through which everything, but everything went, to be carried away, hopefully, at the next high tide.

One of the more amusing stories, certainly true, concerns the village barber who had just died and who had occupied Bosham Castle. The barber had been president of the Bosham Buccaneers, the burgee of which was a shield showing crossed scimitars on an emerald green ground; this had been placed above the doorway of the cottage. As the result, the cottage was given the nickname of The Castle. Not to be outdone, the neighbour decided to

Bosham Castle

call his cottage Bosham Abbey. Many years later, after the 2nd World War, a young man engaged a lady in conversation in a train from London, both bound for Bosham, where the lady lived. During the conversation, it transpired that the young man had been invited down to stay with the surgeon for a weekend's sailing. He was anxious to make a good impression and told his fellow passenger of how worried he was that he might not have brought the

correct clothing for a weekend at Bosham Castle. He had brought his dinner jacket, just in case his hosts were in the habit of changing for dinner! The lady hesitated to tell him that Bosham Castle was no stately home to which he clearly thought he had been invited, but a two-up, two-down tiny cottage in the High Street!

But to go back to 1925 - the landlord of this row of cottages was Captain John Chapman, otherwise known as Uncle John or The Mayor of Bosham. Uncle John was a good landlord and built a balcony on the seaward side of Bosham Castle as well as extending the one next door, Bosham Abbey, for his new tenants. The Ogilvies' were tenants for thirty years, the parents living in the Abbey and the children in the Castle. Sir Heneage Ogilvie later bought both cottages as well as the land across the High Street known as Bull's Field. Heneage on at least one occasion during the 1920's, lent Bosham Abbey to the 'flying' Duchess of Bedford, a keen ornithologist. She used to land her plane in a field near Stumps Farm close to the old school, while the chauffeur brought down her supplies in her Rolls Royce. The first time her chauffeur got lost, looking everywhere for an abbey!

Both cotttages are still owned by his daughters, one of whom, Magdalen Maskell, lives with her husband, Nelson, in Bosham Abbey. During the war years, Jean Ogilvie, married to Dr. Pat Ogilvie, Heneage's son who was serving in the Navy, lived in one of the cottages with her two small children. With one small fire and little coal (but which could be augmented with driftwood collected from the shore), as the only means of heating house and bath water, it must have been one of the more unenviable aspects of living in wartime Bosham. Most of the cottages in the High Street have high steps into both gardens and houses. This is to keep out the sea water during the period of very high spring tides, which occur twice a year.

The Old Town Hall, the last house on the east side of Bosham Lane at Street End, was re-built in 1694 when it was called Copthall. Made of brick and stone, it is thought that the building has Roman foundations; the house has been chopped and changed many times. Originally four or five cottages, in about 1900 two of the cottages were made into one. Prior to that one or more of the cottages may have been used as local council offices, which would account for

The high stepped front door of a house in the High Street

its name. Later, local administration was transferred first to Westbourne Urban District and then to Chichester District

The High Street at the time of the high spring tides. The walls of the two cottages, Bosham Castle and Bosham Abbey are on the right. The Town Hall is the house in the centre

169

Council. In a 1921 Harrods catalogue for the auction of the house, 'Ye Olde Town Hall' is described as one house with two adjoining cottages. The next owner, Dicky Davis, one time Commodore of the Bosham Sailing Club, in about 1927 incorporated the two cottages into the main house. There was a retaining wall along the shore made from oyster shells, while the entrance to the house was up steps from Shore Road. The Holloways bought the house in 1934, and two years later acquired the almost derelict fifth cottage for an extension to the main house. The curtilage was formerly copyhold within the Manor of Bosham. There are many old beams inside the house while the three-way chimney is made from old Roman bricks. At one time it was a Danish guesthouse for visiting sailors and was also used in the 20th century

for Mormon meetings. Brigham Arnold, born in 1856, a member of the well-known Bosham family, was named after the founder of the Mormons, Brigham Young. What looks like a summerhouse, built to blend in with the main building, is in fact the housing for a pump to bring sewage up to the level of the main drainage pipes in Taylors Lane.

Also affected by the high spring tides are the cottages, numbers 4, 5 and 6 Gloucester Terrace, the first houses at the end of Bosham Lane on the east side. Built in the 1700s they had wattle and daub interior walls supported on the outside by bricks. These houses, along with a number of others in the area, were in the Manor of Chidham. This apparent anomaly goes back to the time of Edward the Confessor when the church and part of the Manor of Bosham

Gloucester Terrace in Bosham Lane. The house on the far left was formerly a pub, The Gloucester, then a guest house. It is now a private house

passed to the Bishops of Exeter, whose lands included the church and Manor of Chidham. All the cottages enjoyed the Sussex type of sloping roofs, which went from the top of the building to the ground floor with no break; on the ground floor the occupants had to walk sideways along the passages because of the severely angled roofs. They were built in this manner for warmth and also to give the front rooms more space.

Numbers 4 and 5 have been knocked into one house, now called Gloucester Cottage, while No. 6 is known as Flood Cottage. One window in No. 4 was blocked up after 1696 when the window tax was imposed: anyone with from seven to nine windows had to pay an annual tax of 2s per window (10p); over ten windows and the tax was 4s per window (20p). On the first floor of each cottage there was a coffin hole, created by having easily lifted floorboards. This hole was used for taking coffins up and bodies down; using the steep stairs or step ladder would clearly have been a difficult operation. The hole was probably also used for taking large pieces of furniture such as beds to the upper rooms. The three cottages shared two outside loos (toilets); it was also customary for the tenants to enjoy their weekly ablutions in a tin bath on Saturday afternoons. The water, heated in the laundry coppers, was brought from the dip holes which were positioned down Bosham Lane; there was one outside the present vicarage with another one by the north east corner of the present Bosham Walk. In the gardens of these cottages were found many oyster shells and clay pipes.

Gordon Terrace in Bosham Lane in the early 1900s. In the picture are Annie Coombes, Elsie Follett, Kitty Martin and Winifred White. These houses were originally part of a granary while some of the bricks used were taken from a local windmill

The tenancy of the cottages passed to Kate Woods, née Smart, owner of the boatyard on the High Path, on the death of her parents in 1929 while the ownership of the buildings passed to the 2nd Lord Iveagh, Lord of the Manor of Bosham.

Further up Bosham Lane, the terrace of houses, Numbers. 1,2,3 and 4 Adelaide Terrace were built by Harry Aldous in 1882 on land at one time owned, in part, by Charles Paget Fitzhardinge Berkeley. Aldous subsequently emigrated to Adelaide, Australia, and, it is understood, the cottages were apparently named after his new abode. The land for No. 3 Adelaide Terrace cost £100 and in 1918 the building was sold for £175 to Ernest Layzell who after his unsuccessful attempt to run the bakery with his mother-in-law in what is now Loafers, returned to his old job of railway goods clerk. He died in 1935 leaving the house to his widow. One of his three daughters was Eva Purser who was such a fund of knowledge on Bosham.

The four terraced houses called Gordon Terrace were part of an old granary: some of the bricks which were used for their construction came from a local windmill, possibly the one on the edge of Cut Mill Creek. It is this mill which gave its name to the area now known as Windmill Fields.

Over a window in the Millstream Hotel are inscribed the letters 'WM 1701'; these are thought to be the initials of William Markwick, possibly the builder but certainly the owner of two of the three 17th century workmen's cottages, which were later to form The Grange guesthouse. William's son, Bold, was granted the copyhold of one Cotland in the tithing of Creed 'held by the annual rent of 1/8d' (about 8p). To the east of these three cottages, was The Malt House, though there is no evidence that it was ever used for that purpose. In the Post Office Directory of 1862, John Trevett and Sons, whose family had purchased these properties in 1841, are described as maltsters, (the makers of malt for brewing beer) which may be how that one cottage acquired its name. In 1899 Ernest Trevett is given as the owner of The Grange and Mrs. Elizabeth Trevett as a farmer and coal merchant - there was a coal yard opposite The Grange in front of Brooklyn Cottage. In 1914 Selwyn Lloyd, who had previously lived in The Manor House, bought a fourteen year lease on the building but, in 1919, sub-let it to a Mr. Germain, who ran it as a small guesthouse. Jack Scutt, a coal merchant, is reported to have lived in The Grange in the 1920s and lent land bordering the road to the bowling club. The Montgomerys bought The Grange after the 2nd World War and also ran it as a guesthouse. It was Zoë Jenner who in 1965 bought the business and, after making some additions, changed the name to the Millstream Hotel, obtaining a licence to sell alcoholic drinks with meals. By changing the name of the former guesthouse, the brook, a stream which runs in front of the hotel, is now, quite erroneously, referred as the millstream. In the 1963 brochure of the hotel, bed and breakfast in the summer months cost £1.7s 6d (£1.36p.) while the cost of an electric fire in your room was an extra 1s (5p.). With no central heating, the use of such heating in the winter was probably essential. A further statement in the brochure was 'dogs also are welcomed and allowed in all rooms'!

All three of the cottages to the east of The Grange were also owned by Mrs. Trevett. The most easterly of this group, Burnside, was rented out in 1917 for 5s a week (25p). The tenant told of having the 'loo' (toilet) behind a shed at the bottom of the garden – a wooden seat over a pit! Water for all these three cottages,- Burnside, The Malt House and the barn-like building that juts out, (now the dining room for the hotel) came from a well at the back of the houses. Three years after the death of Mrs. Treveitt in 1930, all three cottages east of the guesthouse were sold while the Malt House and the barn-like section were made into one house; all these building had been connected to main drainage by 1932. After the 2nd World War, the barn-like building between the Malt House and The Grange became the Bosham Sea School with an office and a shop on the ground floor and a classroom upstairs. Here the young would-be sailors were taught the theories of sailing before stepping into a

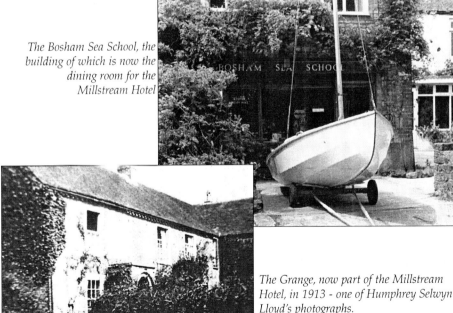

The Bosham Sea School, the building of which is now the dining room for the Millstream Hotel

The Grange, now part of the Millstream Hotel, in 1913 - one of Humphrey Selwyn Lloyd's photographs.

173

floating dinghy. Many of these pupils stayed in the guesthouse or in other houses in the village, while taking the six-day course. The junior pupils had ten-day courses and could stay in the Old Malt House under the care of Mrs. Sandell for £1.11s.0d a day (£1.55p), which included all meals and a packed lunch.

In 1972 the Millstream was sold to Peter Stevens, a London wine merchant who also bought Church Farm opposite. He too enlarged the hotel by building an extension on the western end so cleverly that it is difficult to tell the old from the new. Four years later he sold the hotel to the Wild family, who in 1980 purchased the Malt House (including the former sea school) and Burnside incorporating all three into the hotel. In 1999 the hotel purchased the thatched bungalow, Waterside, next door. Now an AA and RAC accredited hotel, the Millstream has also received the Gold Award for exceptional comfort,

hospitality and service from the English Tourism Council – the only award made in West Sussex. So in three hundred years, the cottages of 1700 have become one of the leading country hotels in southern England. However, history does not relate whether, with all the alterations over the years, once a year the ghost of a dog still appears during the night in room number five. He is reported to sit on the bed for a while, looking at the occupant, then vanish. There are also stories that staff have seen people walking through the hotel who are not recognised as guests, but they too mysteriously float away as fast as they appear.

Opposite the Millstream Hotel is the 18th century Church Farm, Bosham Lane, of which the earliest public records show James Hayllar as the owner in 1849. Originally a small cottage, the building was enlarged and today gives the appearance of being a very attractive Georgian fronted

Church Farm House, Bosham Lane, in the 1980s

farmhouse. In 1861 it was owned by John Trevett, maltster, grocer and coal merchant, who leased Church Farm for 10s 8d (about 53 p.) to Madame Idle (née Amelia Collins) where she remained for ten years. In 1920 E.M. & K.G. Trevett sold some land west of Church Farm House, to miller George Brown; four years later the same two Trevett brothers sold another seven acres to the miller for £1190; in 1930 the house was sold to Agatha Coldham.

Selwyn Lloyd, in his pamphlet 'A Thumbnail Sketch of old Bosham' wrote that in the early 1900s, Mr. Trevett spoke of how, when digging in the garden of this house, he often found betrothal rings 'which in the old days were frequently buried on the hands of the persons who had worn them during life'. This suggests that there was a burial ground in the immediate area. There are references to the discovery of foundations which could be those of a small chapel or charnel house (a building for placing the bones of the dead). After the closure of the mill on the Quay in 1936 George Brown's son used the land and buildings which his father had retained, to run a small electric mill where, until 1954, he ground animal feeds. The lovely old

The barn which formed part of Church Farm was destroyed in the 1960s in order to widen the road. In the distance is the Grange guest house, now the Millstream Hotel

The Millstream Hotel today

175

barn, which was next door to Church Farm was knocked down in the late 1960s to ease the traffic congestion on this corner of Bosham Lane. The name Church Farm suggests that, at some time, this property had also been owned by the Church.

It is not known when Loafers in Bosham Lane, was built; it was originally two 18th century cottages which appear on a map of 1778. A tithe map of 1839 shows the appropriators as the Dean and Chapter of Chichester, a previous owner having been Edward Bennett; another of the many properties he owned. The 1841 tithe map shows the property as part of the estate of the College and Rectory of Bosham. It was about this time that the house was known as Rose Cottage and was the village bakery. The bakery Rose Cottage may have been an alehouse frequented by oyster fishermen at some time. With yeast a common ingredient of both bread and ale, the brewing of ale could have been a sideline to the bakery. In the 1861 census George and Sarah Purver are listed as bakers and the address as Rose Cottage. George died in 1888 and his widow Sarah continued to run the bakery with the help of her son-in-law, Ernest Layzell. By 1899 Sarah

Ye Olde Bosham Bakery in the early 1900s when this house was called Rose Cottage

Ye Olde Bosham Tea Shoppe in about 1948

was forced to sell the bakery to the Chichester brewery, Sparkes. Around 1919 or 1920, the business was sold again to Arthur Miles Colebourne, who with his brother-in-law Len Carpenter, was running the brewery. Len was later to run the newsagents in Station Road. In 1948 the building was renovated and converted into a tearoom. Not long after that it was sold again to become a private house now called Loafers.

Critchfield House is a 17th century building in Bosham Lane almost opposite Critchfield Road. When the house was being refurbished in the early 1980s, evidence of Roman occupation was found under the kitchen floor. There were also Saxon stones found similar to those which can be seen in the church today while the foundations of the house suggest that they may be those from an earlier monastery which stood here. The psychic friend of the owner, staying soon after these renovations were complete, found the atmosphere in the building to be very friendly and she described seeing figures looking like Trappist monks, walking through the house, a description similar to those seen in the church by Pen Rycroft (See page 213). In Place names of Sussex the name Lucia atte Crich was shown in the Sussex Subsidy Rolls of 1332 and this could have been the origin of the name Critchfield. Critch could be a derivative of the word 'Cross' also suggesting an earlier ecclesiastical connection.

Selwyn Lloyd writes in his diaries 'For some hundreds of years there was another monastery in Bosham which was a very important ecclesiastical centre…on that part of Bosham called Critchfield. The foundations of a very ancient building can still be seen there … in the lower part of the walls of the

Loafers the former bakery/tearoom as it is today

Above: A 17th century barn, photographed in August1985. It was part of Church Farm House but is now surrounded by newer houses & difficult to see.
Below: Critchfield House, at one time a guest house and hotel, but now a private house

house known as Hole in the Wall'. This building, next door to Critchfield House, was the stables and coachman's cottage for the main house. In a schedule of the conveyances from 1853-87 the house was part of the Manor of Bosham, owned by the Berkeleys. Amelia Idle leased this house for her mother, Amelia Collins, in about 1861 . A conveyance of August 1887 shows that the Rev. William August St. John Dearsley, Clerk in Holy Orders, bought from Mercy Richardson, widow and a copyhold tenant of the Manor, 'all that dwellinghouse & garden ' – this refers to Critchfield House. Was Mr. Dearsley the male friend of the young lady who lived in Broadstream Cottage and the father of the little girl? The cleric's arrival in Bosham was not popular and he was regularly subject to 'rough music' - the banging of trays, pots and pans outside his house in the evening. He had to call the police and the noise stopped. Later he was to become a very popular and much loved figure in the village. In 1914, when the executors of Mr. Dearsley sold the property, the details referred to one dwellinghouse with coach house, stable, outbuildings, yard, garden and a coachman's cottage. This was not very different from the description of the property in the Court Rolls of 1822 when it is recorded as being 'one dwelling house and orchard plus garden and one acre of Forrep'. (A 'Forrep' is a word peculiar to the Manor of Bosham and means assart land, i.e. forest land cleared to make it available for cultivation.)

In 1941, the Rev. A. L. Chatfield, the vicar of Bosham, bought Critchfield House and was to use it as the vicarage until 1950. The Army had commandeered the official vicarage, now known as Walton House, at the beginning of the 2nd World War. Mr. J.F. Wills was the next owner and, with his sister, ran a very comfortable and simple guesthouse. At a time when it was difficult to 'eat out', it was possible to order in advance and enjoy a very pleasant dinner in Critchfield House. A later owner enlarged the guesthouse and converted it into a small hotel, renaming it the Viking Hotel. Bed and breakfast in the hotel in the 1970s cost £3 per person per day from April to September and in the winter months the price was only £2 15s 0d (£2.75). The brochure for the hotel at the time reads 'This hotel is tastefully furnished and facilities include full central heating, licensed restaurant, bar, TV room, coffee room, car park'.

Recently, many of the additions made in the 1970s and 80s have been removed and it is now a Grade II listed private house. Next door is the former coach house previously known as Critchfield Cottage. In 1921 this building was entirely reconstructed into a modern homestead and renamed The Hole in the Wall. It was owned for many years by the Shippam family of the world famous Shippam's paste factory in Chichester. In the early 2000s, this house was completely rebuilt internally but the original roadside façade was retained.

Almost certainly one of the many mills in Bosham referred to in

Domesday, is Cut Mill. The present building is of the 15th century when water from the River Cut turned the wheel. The mill ceased operations in about 1918-19, the last miller being Amos Wakeford. It was bought, restored (at a cost, it is believed, of about £50,000) and converted into a substantial house by Fran Tennyson-Jesse, the novelist, and her husband, Harold Marsh Harwood (the playright H.M. Harwood but always known as Tottie). In 1922 the newly-weds converted the Henry VII mill house into a home, retaining as much as possible of the old milling machinery. Over the front door there are the figures of a little man and woman, half in and half out of a stone weather house. Carved on a table underneath these figures are George Herbert's words 'Building is a sweet impoverish, HMH and FTJ 1922'. The Harwoods were great entertainers and amongst their annual guests were Sir Lewis Casson, the actor and producer, and his wife, the actress, Dame Sybil Thorndike. Here the Harwoods were to stay until 1937 when they sold the house to Percy Harry Thompson, otherwise known as Percy Honri of concert fame.

Only a few yards down the road from Cut Mill is the former Neptune House, now called Newells House, which was the 19th century coach house and stables to a grander building nearby, thought to be Cut Mill House – now demolished. In the 1930s it was renovated to become a five bedroomed house in the style of a Roman palace with classical columns and statues. Today it is a whitewashed simple elegant house with the River Cut running through the extensive gardens. Noël Coward is reputed to have visited the house frequently and used a small flat within to do some of his writing.

At the other end of the parish from Cut Mill is Furzefield. In 1919, Winifred Allen, bought from Frederick Sadler, a Chichester grain

Furzefield House built by Lady Allen in 1919 on the ruins of the former brickmakers cottages

merchant, the western half of what is today known as Bosham Hoe. This included the old brickworks, which had closed down in that year. On the foundations of the two brick-makers cottages, Lady Allen built the five bedroomed Furzefield House with spectacular views down Chichester Harbour to Hayling Island and the Isle of Wight. On the foundations of the second ruined cottage, she created the three-bedroomed Furzefield Cottage. While building Furzefield, Sir Hugh and Lady Allen, lived on board the Thames barge Elsie tied alongside Furzefield jetty. The story goes that a uniformed maid was to be seen each morning, washing down the decks and filling the dustbins with the household rubbish –

tipping overboard was strictly forbidden. In 1923 Lady Allen sold the whole of Furzefield and the surrounding land to Rose Richards, only to buy it back again in 1946, by which time Lady Allen owned the whole of the Bosham Hoe peninsula except for the plots of land she had sold for development. In 1947, Lady Allen sold Furzefield House with a few acres of land, to Commander Philip Gick and his wife, who brought up a family of three daughters and a son here. Aylmer Gick was an architect and keen gardener who designed a number of the houses on the Hoe. Today the family still own the house though Rear-Admiral Gick, as he became, and his wife Aylmer have both died.

After a storm in 1959, the yacht Satyre ended up against the wall of the Town Hall

1. *The Swan Inn in the early 1980s. It was a coaching inn on the main road between Chichester and Portsmouth. During this time it was also the local Post Office*

2. *The Crown Inn in Walton Lane in the 1900s*

3. *Crede Cottages, part of which building was the Crown Inn.*

4. *Walton Inn, demolished in the 1950s, had been used by foreign labourers brought in to help with the harvest and who slept rough in the fields behind the inn. The barn beyond still exists*

CHAPTER 13
Ale is the Drink of Kings & Sailors

The Romans started the concept of inns as lodging houses where travellers could get food and a bed for the night. The symbol for such a facility was either a vine or ivy twisted around a pole outside the building. The Saxons continued the custom, but most of those built for this function were made of wood so the buildings did not survive for long. The responsibility for giving hospitality to travellers then passed to the monks – most monasteries had their guests rooms where travellers could obtain a palliasse for the night, food and drink, the latter the locally brewed ale, for water was not deemed safe to drink. In the early 19th century when the population of the village was around eight hundred souls there were no less than eleven pubs (public houses) in the parish of Bosham. While there are only three left in the village itself some of the others, though still being used for their original purpose, are now in the parishes of Chidham and Fishbourne. The rest are private houses.

The first pub in Bosham was almost certainly The Anchor in the High Street. Liquid refreshment, principally of ales and beers, has been served from the present building since about the 1700s, but it is thought that there was originally a mediaeval alehouse on the site – as a seaport, it would have been very strange if there had not been some place in this vicinity where sailors could quench their thirst. During renovations, an old Tudor wall was found in the building. Officially it is called The Anchor Bleu and this is believed to originate from the Royal Navy who had an Admiral of the Blue Fleet (the Home Fleet) and one of the Red Fleet, but how this came to be associated with The Anchor it is difficult to know. Until recently local pubs were a form of club, where local men gathered regularly with their mates for a pint, usually on Friday and Saturday nights. Few pubs offered food, such as they do today. Here the men, for it was not considered quite proper for respectable ladies to be seen drinking in pubs, played such games as darts and shove halfpenny, competing with teams from other local alehouses. Situated as it is on the shores of the village, The Anchor would have catered not only for local and visiting seamen but landlubbers as well. It was no doubt the centre of the local smuggling ring, where carrier and pedlar could meet. There are supposed to be underground passages from The Anchor to the church, to the monks'

1. Bosham Lane showing the inn sign for the Gloucester Inn on the far left

2. Robert Martin, (bearded) keeper of the Ship Inn in the High Street in about 1882

The doorstep of the Old Ship

4. The High Street showing the Anchor and two doors away, the Old Ship (Photo Garland Collection)

3. The Berkeley Arms in about 1850. Although the painting shows the thatched building as the pub, the Berkeley Arms of today more closely resembles the building on the right of the picture

184

cells, under the Manor House and up to the main road, from where the contraband could be dispersed into the countryside. In the 19th century, the Courts of the Manor of Chidham were held here while during the 1860s, one of the rooms was being used as a local coroner's court. For many years the Bosham Sailing Club had some of its meetings in one of the upstair rooms.

Two doors away from The Anchor was The Ship, again a spot where there could have been a building used as a hostelry for a few centuries. The present building was originally three cottages forming part of a block of 18th century two-storied houses. At the turn of the nineteenth and twentieth centuries, the two Martin brothers, John and Robert were, respectively, the landlords of The Anchor and of the Ship. During the last war, The Ship was an Officers Club, used principally by the Royal Air Force personnel stationed at nearby Thorney Island and at the front line fighter aircraft station at Tangmere. Many well-known servicemen were members, while in 1944, Rex Whistler, the very well known artist, painter and illustrator of books, drew a mural on the wall, depicting some of the local characters, using any medium he could lay his hand on at the time – pencils, crayons and even lipstick. A lieutenant in the 2nd (Armoured) Battalion Welsh Guards, Whistler was stationed near Hambledon, Hampshire, awaiting embarkation to France after the D-Day landings in Normandy. During those ten days, Whistler with some of his fellow officers, were given permission to visit the Ship Club and it was while in the club that he painted this mural. The battalion left for Normandy on the 29th June and Rex was killed nineteen days later, so this mural would appear to have been his last work. The mural was beginning to disintegrate badly, so the owners of The Old Ship (now a private house), have found a conservator who

The mural on the wall of the Old Ship, probably the last work of Rex Whistler who was killed in Normandy in 1944 about ten days after working on this painting

has restored it. It has been a lengthy specialist job but it is now back in its original position looking as near its previous state as possible.

A few doors up from Street End, at the southern end of Bosham Lane, is Gloucester House, formerly The Gloucester Arms, named, it is thought, after the county in which the Berkeley family, who were Lords of the Manor of Bosham for four hundred years, had their seat. Here, about a hundred years ago, the Bosham Blackbirds, a male singing group met regularly. The practice night was usually Thursday and of a summer evening, when windows and doors were open, the sounds could be heard all over the village and, according to those around at the time, produced a wonderful sound. The Blackbirds put on regular concerts locally. In 1855 Edward Trevett, a ships' captain, leased the building and in 1862 he became the innkeeper. By 1881, Edward Collins, aged 29, a member of the Collins family, was the innkeeper of The Gloucester. After it ceased to be a pub, it became a guest house run by Ethel Frogbrook and her two daughters. It is now a private house

Another pub is The Berkeley Arms, also named after the Lords of the Manor of Berkeley Castle in Gloucestershire. The original pub was a thatched building to the west of the present one. This was probably burnt down, for in a 19th century sketch of the 'Berks' the present building resembles the house next door to the thatched one.

Thomas Collins is shown as the landlord in Kelly's directories of 1862 and 1874. He was the son of John and Sophia Collins and a nephew of Amelia Collins, afterwards Madame Idle. (See Chapter 11).

The pubs did not usually have any form of overnight accommodation. The inns, descendants of the Roman ones, were those which provided a bed and food for travellers. Such a one is The White Swan on the main road. This inn was used as a staging post during the short period of the horse-drawn coaches that ran between Portsmouth, Brighton and London in the early 19th century. It was during those days that the post office had an branch here. Here in 1862 Williams Collins, another son of John and Sophia, was the landlord.

Of the other pubs – The Benbow on Gosportside, possibly Loafers in Bosham Lane, the Crown, now Crede Cottages, and Parkers Pound both in Walton Lane, are all private houses. The Walton in Walton Lane, used by itinerant seasonal workers, has been pulled down and four houses built on the site. The Globe, now a private house, and the Black Boy are in Fishbourne parish while the Old House at Home is in Chidham.

Today the three remaining pubs in the village all provide food and, in fine weather during the summer months particularly, find themselves popular hostelries.

CHAPTER 14

'Society goes on and on and on' Robert Graves

It is difficult to identify the oldest club or organisation still in operation in the village. The oldest club must be the Football Club started in 1901 and still going strong, with the Tennis and Cricket Clubs following in 1902. Tennis is still played in the village, but there is no longer a club. The Cricket Club is still very active. Then came the Sailing Club in 1907 and in 1911 the Old English Bowling Club, which met in the Berkeley Arms with the bowling greens next door. Between the two world wars the Women's Institute was started in 1921 and the Horticultural Society during the 1930s. During the 20th century, many other clubs and organisations were started, some to flourish, others to disappear. Below are the histories of some of them.

THE WOMENS INSTITUTE

On the 21st November, 1921, on the initiative of Mrs. Rochford-Wade, wife of the then vicar of Bosham, a group of ladies met in the Foresters' Hall, a building beside and part of the White Swan Inn on the Main Road, to investigate the possibility of forming a Women's Institute in the village. Mrs. Rochford-Wade became the first president. Among those who formed the first committee were Miss Heaver (later to become president); Mrs. Follett, wife of the owner of Follett's Stores in the High Street; Miss Ruby Brown, sister of farmer George Brown; Mrs. Henshall, wife of the artist who did the drawings for the Rev. Kenneth MacDermott's book 'Bosham Church: Its History and Antiquities'; Mrs. Hickman, wife of the blacksmith at Apps Shipyard, Quay Meadow; Mrs. Richardson, wife of the grocer who built what became Broadbridge Stores in Bosham Lane and which is now an estate agent's office and shop.

The first committee meeting was held at the Vicarage on 7th December 1921 and the first official meeting was in the Foresters Hall on the 15th December, when sixty-one ladies were enrolled as members of the Bosham Women's Institute. It is believed the annual subscription was 2s (10p.) . A cup of tea cost one penny, with another penny for a piece of cake. The Institute held meetings alternately between the Foresters' and the Congregational Church halls (now the United Reformed Church) until the village hall was built in 1925.

Among the foundation members was Mrs. Carpenter, wife of the sub-postmaster and newsagent in Station Road and mother of Joyce Stant, who, some sixty years later, was to be Chairman of the West Sussex Federation of Women's Institutes. Alongside the newsagent was a tin and aluminium building known as The Pavilion, also owned by the Carpenters, which was used for village dances, jumble sales and – on some occasions – W.I. committee meetings.

The subjects for the meetings held in the early days give some idea of the original aims of the W.I. – namely to educate the young country wives of the day to meet and learn how to be better mothers and housekeepers. The new president persuaded her husband, the vicar, to be one of the first speakers, when at the meeting on 23rd March, 1922, he spoke on the subject 'Our Food'. Other subjects for the monthly lectures were 'Nursing & Child Welfare', 'Re-covering an umbrella', 'Demonstration on stuffing chairs and replacing springs', 'What to do before the doctor arrives' (by the Matron of the Royal West Sussex Hospital), 'Old turned into new' and 'How to save work in spring cleaning'. For competitions there were 'The best supper for 1s' (5p), 'a home-made night-dress for 5/-' (25p), and 'The best school lunch for 6d'. (2½ p) won by Mrs. Follett, the grocer's wife.

It was not many months before it was proposed that the W.I. in conjunction with the Football Club, should look into the possibility of building a hall-cum-meeting place for the benefit of the village. A fête was held in the garden of Broadbridge House, home of the new president, Miss Heaver, a member of one of the local farming families. Over £160 was raised to start a building fund; other donations followed from individuals and organisations. An architect, Mr. Whitehead, drew up plans and in April 1924 a quarter acre site, situated where the present village hall now stands, was purchased from farmer George Brown at a cost of £1 per foot (0.33 metre). As the Institute itself could not own property, trustees were appointed to form a building committee which consisted mainly of W.I. and Football club members as well as George Brown and the architect. The foundation stone of the hall was laid in the autumn of 1924 and the formal opening was on Friday, March 17th 1925. The cost of the building was £250. At a special meeting of the W.I on 6th March 1924, a resolution was passed that when the final deed was drawn up there should be a clause prohibiting the sale of intoxicating liquor on the premises. This was passed unanimously! This clause does not apply today.

A tennis court was laid down beside the hall and in October 1925 a library was opened. This hall stood until 1996 when, with the financial help of the County, District, Parish and Sports Councils and the Lottery Fund, as well as other public bodies and local residents, a total of over £300,000 was raised to build a new hall on the site of

1. The Broadbridge House housemaid and parlourmaid

2. Broadbridge House, the scene of money raising fêtes to build the first village hall

3. Wall hanging made by the WI sewing group 'A Thousand Years of Bosham 1086-1986'

4. Mrs Guy (president) with Peggy Watson (secretary) and the treasurer at a WI meeting in the early 1950s

5. Making tea at the first WI meeting in the new village hall in May 1996

6. WI birthday party in 1991 attended by Mrs Joyce Stant (née Carpenter) Chairman of the Federation of West Sussex

the old one. This hall is now managed by a Village Hall Management Committee (Trustees) made up of a representative from the Parish Council and each of the various clubs, groups and organisations who use it. This new hall would have cost a great deal more but for the fact that the site was already available as a result of the W.I. land purchase in 1924.

In those early years a Tennis Club, Folk Dance Club, drama, needlework and ballroom dancing groups were formed and cookery classes held, some of which continue to this day. There was a weekly market selling local produce on Friday mornings at Pedlar's garage (where Bosham Walk is now situated) which continued until after the 2nd World War. A local W.I. Market re-opened in 1974 when on Friday mornings long queues formed outside the village hall, so successful was this venture. Unfortunately it closed in 1991, not for lack of customers but as a result of a shortage of cooks and growers to stock the various stalls.

By October 1927 there were over one hundred members, while some fourteen years later there were no less than a hundred and fifty. Bosham W.I. was a strong force during the 1939-45 war when members grew, preserved and distributed food to the local towns, while the village itself was expected to be self-supporting. Evacuee mothers, billeted in the village, were invited to join the Institute. The Institute acquired a canning machine which enabled members to preserve fruit and vegetables, while sugar was distributed to members to make jams and chutneys – in 1940 over two tons of jam were made and sold. As it was important that the canned fruit tins be cooled quickly, ladies were to be seen scurrying down Bosham Lane from the village hall carrying fishnets filled with steaming cans which were dunked into the brook to cool. (There must have been some surprised overheated fish in the brook on these occasions!). In 1942, two hundredweight of rosehips were collected, largely by schoolchildren, for making into syrup, an excellent source of vitamin C for the youngsters. The W.I. supervised school lunches in the village hall, making hot home-made soup in the winter for a penny a cup and cool drinks in the summer to have with the lunches the children brought from home; quite a problem for mothers with the meagre food rations.

In August 1945, the W.I. organised a tea party in the village for eight hundred adults and children to celebrate VJ Day.

Different groups for various activities have remained, come and gone, but the sewing group has continued through all these years – curtains were made by them for both old and new halls on more than one occasion. In 1947, a scrapbook was entered for a County Federation competition of village scrapbooks, when Bosham W.I. came second. In 1986, to celebrate 1,000 years of the village – Bosham was listed as one of the wealthiest manors in England in the Domesday Book of 1086 – the sewing group made an embroidered wall hanging showing buildings as well as the flora and fauna to be seen in the village in that year. This now hangs in the village hall as well as the Parish Millennium Map made by the Art Group in 2000.

Other groups which have been formed besides art, are book lovers, discussion, swimming, drama, walking, craft (the new name for the sewing group) and music. After completion of the new hall in 1996, the membership rose again. A popular and remunerative fund raiser, replacing the annual jumble sales, has been the guided tours of the village followed by cream teas, for groups visiting the village.

Every year in November, the Institute has a celebratory birthday party. For the Institute's 80th birthday in 2001, a special lunch was held in the new hall when six past presidents were invited. A few weeks before, Ann Webb at the 2001 Annual Council Meeting had been elected County Chairman of the West Sussex Federation of Women's Institutes.

The Bosham W.I. still continues to be a powerful voice in the village. In 1922 it was one of the very few organisations in existence and was thus a very important aspect of local life. Today at the turn of the 21st century, it has much competition from the Flower Club, Horticultural Society, Cricket and Football Clubs as well as many other organisations in the vicinity; nevertheless it continues to flourish.

The village hall then and now

BOSHAM SAILING CLUB

In 1907, a small building known as 'Paddy's Studio' on Shore Road, a few yards west of the Anchor, saw the beginning of the Bosham Sailing Club. Originally used as stables and then by an artist, today 'Paddy's Studio' is known as Littlecroft and forms part of Canute Cottage. The building was given and suitably furnished by Mr. E.K. Chapman-Collis, who was an active club member for over fifty years and who became the club's first president The clubroom was open from 10 a.m. to 10.30 p.m. daily where, during the winter months books and games were provided and in the summer sailing matches were arranged when the starting gun was fired out of the window of the clubroom. Membership was open to anyone over the age of eighteen and the subscription was one penny ($^1/_2$p today) a week with no entrance fee. The first honorary secretary and treasurer was Glyn Martin, the son of George Martin who, in 1872, had eloped with one of the then vicar's daughters, Charlotte Sophia Mitchell. The more official club meetings were held in the Anchor, the landlord of which, Mr. H.L. Hull, became the treasurer from 1921-37. These meetings continued to be held in the Anchor until the 1970s when the little cottage attached to the old mill was incorporated into the main clubhouse and provided the necessary additional space. In 1927, a clubroom was established in the Raptackle on the Quay with a starting platform on the upper floor and storage for dinghies underneath.

In 1947, after the end of the 2nd World War, a motor gunboat, MGB614, which had seen much action in the English Channel during the war, was purchased as a club headquarters and moored alongside the Quay. For nine years this vessel provided dining facilities, sleeping accommodation for a steward and his wife as well as bunks for up to twenty members. In 1956 the Lord of the Manor, the 2nd Lord Iveagh, granted the club a fifty-year lease of the mill on the Quay for their headquarters and clubhouse; he charged a peppercorn rent of £50 per annum, The management of the club undertook responsibility for converting and maintaining the interior of the building. In 1992, a new lease on a commercial basis was re-negotiated with the Manor of Bosham Ltd; this included the use of part of the Raptackle and a large dinghy park.

From then on the Club never looked back. Membership increased and regular sailing races were held, but the lack of water at low tide in this part of the harbour severely restricted dinghy racing. In about 1960, the Beale family, who owned Cobnor House as well as a many acres of farmland on the Chidham Peninsula, offered the club a lease of some land at the head of Bosham Creek, where there was deep water available at all stages of the tide. A starting platform, a pavilion and lavatories were also built here for the use of the club. Although the size of boats which can be launched over the Cobnor hard is limited, these facilities enabled the expansion of dinghy racing together with the ability to host open and national dinghy meetings.

One of the major events of the Club's year is the annual regatta which, except for the war years, has been held in Bosham since 1908. It is on record that there were regattas held in the harbour prior to 1900, when the organisers were the customs' officers who started the races from the Customs House at Itchenor; the participants were the local fishermen of the fishing fleets from all

the harbour villages. The first recorded regatta held in Bosham was on Thursday 17th September 1908, particulars for which could be obtained, according to the posters, from the 'Hon Secs, Ye Old Anchor Inn, Bosham'. The first race was for the Bosham Challenge Trophy for 'bona-fide Bosham Fishing Boats. If C.B. [centreboard] keels, to be fixed up or down and sealed. Masts not to exceed 20 ft.' [just over 6 metres] There were other races for a 'Bona-fide cruising yacht handicap', 'A Handicap Sailing Race for Pleasure Boats' and a 'Ladies Double-

An aerial view of October 1949 of the Church and Quay. Alongside the Quay is the MGB which was used as the club HQ for nine years

1. Emsworth one design & 12m. sharpie boats alongside the quay at Bosham Sailing Club Regatta of about 1935

2. The Committee Boat anchored off the quay for the start of the rowing race at the 1913 Regatta

3. Ella Minter, Commodore, presenting prizes at the 1951 Regatta

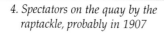

4. Spectators on the quay by the raptackle, probably in 1907

5. Spectators at the 1912 Regatta - one of Humph Selwyn Lloyd's photographs

6. The greasy pole competition at the 1913 regatta

handed Rowing Race'. (It is understood that the ladies' boating apparel was inspected by the committee before such races!) The Blue Hungarian Band was in attendance while Lady Gifford, wife of the Lord of the Manor, distributed the prizes. In the evening there was an 'Illuminated Fête, Concert and Dancing'. Today the events of 'Walking on the Greasy Pole' or 'Tug of War in Boats' are no longer featured in the programme!

From then on, except for the years of the two world wars, the regattas became an annual event, initially held on Thursdays, which was half day closing for the shops, and the school closed to enable the children to take part. Today, the dates for all the regattas of all the clubs in Chichester Harbour are decided by the Federation of Chichester Harbour Clubs so that there shall be no clashing of dates for fixtures. After the 1st World War in 1920, the regattas were held under the name of the Bosham and Itchenor Sailing Clubs. However in the 1922 regatta programme the words 'and Itchenor' were crossed out. From then on Itchenor Sailing Club held their own regattas at weekends, for unlike Bosham whose members were largely local, Itchenor was beginning to draw its membership from further afield, particularly London. By 1920, Bosham had become the yachting centre of the harbour.

Today the Club has a strong cruiser section, with rallies throughout the year, weekly dinghy racing as well as a lively junior section. The area where pigs were once housed has been turned into a patio for observing and imbibing, while the little cottage attached to the old mill is now the Club office. In 2005 the annual membership fees range from £50 for a cadet (under 18 years) to £210 for those over twenty-six years of age; a far cry from the one penny a week subscription of 1907. The membership of the Club in 1947 was two hundred and fifty; today it is eighteen hundred and there is a waiting list. In 2007, the Club will celebrate its centenary.

The Admiral of Bosham (Henry Blandford) with the 2nd Lord Iveagh & other seafaring locals at the 1951 Regatta

The Admiral of Bosham's coxswain & crew at a regatta in the early 1900s

195

BOSHAM ASSOCIATION

The Bosham Association was formed in 1963 principally as a result of the hard work of Admiral Sir Kaye Edden, who was very concerned when a large housing estate was built behind The Grange now the Millstream Hotel. This Association was to be a ginger group to monitor planning applications with a view to preventing any over-development in the village. The first meeting was held in July 1963 in the Berkeley Arms and consisted of seven people, including Frank Parham, Chairman at the time of the Parish Council, Ella Minter, Parish and District Councillor and former President of Bosham Women's Institute, as well as five other leading residents of the village.

Within a year, the Bosham Association had made itself felt by calling for a speed limit on Taylors Lane! In the early 1970s the newly formed Chichester Harbour Conservancy under the Chairmanship of Vice Admiral Sir Geoffrey Thistleton-Smith wished to have a 'honey pot' viewpoint and picnic site on the edge of the harbour. The only suitable site was, it was thought, at the end of Smugglers Lane, adjacent to Ferry Path. The Conservancy plan was to compulsory purchase a field to the west of Ferry Path as a car park for two hundred and fifty cars. Picnic tables and benches were to be installed on the shore to enable the general public to have access to the water, swim and observe the yacht racing organised from Itchenor Sailing Club as well as all the other boating activities. The Bosham Association circularised every house in the village asking residents to come to a public protest meeting in the village hall. There was standing room only! The members of the Harbour Conservancy as well as officers from the County Council were told by local residents that that particular point in the harbour was highly dangerous for swimming, that Itchenor Sailing Club did not start their races from the clubhouse, but further down the harbour which could not be seen from this point. Also it was pointed out that Taylors, Hoe, Smugglers and Lower Hone Lanes were not suitable for the amount of traffic envisaged. The Harbour Conservancy abandoned the idea, but it gave the Bosham Association a great deal of favourable publicity which increased their membership.

In 1968, thanks to the initiative of Joan Hunt, the secretary, an historical and archaeological section was started. One of the first sites on which they worked was in the garden of the Mill House, immediately west of the church, with the permission of Lady Brigid Ness, daughter of the 2nd Lord Iveagh, a previous Lord of the Manor. The 'dig' was under the supervision of Mrs. Margaret Rule, at the time Curator of the Roman Palace at Fishbourne, with the help of Dr. Marie Clough and forty-eight volunteers. They established that there had been occupation in the immediate area over the previous nine hundred years. Also, a number of ancient artefacts were found within the building and grounds. In 1973, this group did another dig during alterations to the present Millstream Hotel, when an eleventh or twelfth century Hickstead pot was found.

Another project undertaken by three members of the committee of the Bosham Association, namely Derek Coombe, Peter Price and Peter Stern, was the production of a comprehensive report on the serious flooding in the village. In 1993-4 and again in 2000-1 the Bosham peninsula was virtually cut off south of the main road by severe flooding. There was a complete breakdown of the sewage drainage, man-hole covers were lifted by the force of the water and many homes were seriously damaged by the flood waters. This report was adopted by the Bosham Parish Council and the Association's team congratulated on a very excellent and comprehensive analysis of the flooding. Local services have been hard at work to act on the recommendations, over 90% of which were completed by 2004.

Today the Bosham Association, entirely non-political, carries out numerous minor village improvements and coerces the authorities into undertaking the major ones. It also keeps a watching brief on all planning applications for the village, thus fulfilling its aim 'to maintain, protect and enhance the character and amenities of Bosham and neighbourhood'.

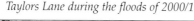

Taylors Lane during the floods of 2000/1

FOOTBALL CLUB

The Bosham Football Club was formed in 1901 when the first match played by members of the newly formed Club took place on 14th December of that year – Bosham was beaten 2-6 by the Chichester Juniors. The first Annual General Meeting of the new Club was held on August 26th 1902 when Lord Gifford, VC, Lord of the Manor, was elected the first president while the new vicar of Bosham, Rev. K.H. MacDermott one of the vice-presidents. The annual subscription was 2/- (10p.) For the Club colours the members chose red which is still used to this day.

In 1903 the Chichester and Bognor District League was formed, the Bosham Club being one of the founder

The junior football team in 1932

1933-34 junior football team

members. Their first success came in 1907 when the club won the League Championship; a celebratory annual dinner was held in the Anchor when a bell which is incorporated into the club badge, was suspended from the ceiling and the members all wore red ties and red buttonholes. The Club also won the Champions' Championships in 1912-13. In December 1912 a benefit match against a League representative team was played at Bosham in aid of the fund for the widows of the Bosham fishermen who had been drowned earlier in the year.

The Bosham Football Club, in 1925, joined forces with the Women's Institute in building the first village hall on land purchased from Farmer George Brown. Between 1913 and 1949, which covered the two world wars, it had been a struggle to maintain the continuity of the Club although, in 1936, the Bosham Parish Council had purchased from Farmer Brown the recreation ground, behind the village hall. This has remained the home of the Football Club ever since. In 1970 a new clubhouse was built, while 1972 saw the formation of the Bosham Cygnets for young people. The Cygnets did not survive after 1998 but in 2004 an under-eleven team was formed, so it is hoped, with more young talent coming forward, the Club will continue long into the new century.

1912-1913 Bosham football club team

199

CRICKET CLUB

Humphrey Selwyn Lloyd wrote in his diaries of how in 1902 he started a Cricket Club in Bosham, of which he was for many years the first president and treasurer. The first match took place in a field which is now the site of Sunnyway, off Bosham Lane. There are photographs of cricket matches, Ladies versus Gentlemen in 1901 – whether these have been incorrectly dated or whether there were matches here before the formation of a club it is difficult to say. There is reference to the Bosham teams playing matches in Brighton and on other grounds. In 1905 a piece of ground for a cricket pitch alongside what is now Bosham Farm Shop was lent by James Toop, described as a sheepman. Later it is also recorded that James Toop of Southwood Farm, farmer and landowner, put a large field south-east of Little Gosport at the disposal of the Cricket Club, where a pitch was laid, a pavilion built and from the money taken at the gate, all the necessary items bought for a cricket club. But there is an entry in the Chichester Observer of July 1938 which reads 'At the meeting held at the Swan Inn, the new Bosham Cricket Club was formed. Mr. B. Merritt was elected hon. secretary and the Club played their first official match when they were entertained by the Chichester Theological College.' Sometime in the 1960s the Club moved to behind Bosham Farm Shop, possibly back to where they had been in 1905, leasing the ground from one of the local landowners, the Heavers. Cricketers are becoming more robust with the result that balls are being hit harder and further, so cricket matches became a hazard to customers entering the farm shop and the Club was forced to find a new pitch.

Plans are presently being made to build a new modern cricket ground and pavilion in a field west of Delling Lane not far from the Bowling Club greens. Planning permission has been granted so it is hoped that when the necessary funds have been raised, it will not be too long before there are, once again, first class cricket facilities available for both sexes and all ages in the village.

Ladies & Gentlemen's Cricket team, May 1901

TENNIS CLUB

A Tennis Club was started in Bosham in about 1902, to which Humphrey Selwyn Lloyd refers in his diaries. There was a court at the Manor House, where Selwyn Lloyd lived with his family until 1919, so a tennis club may well have been one of the many organisations in which he had a hand. The Women's Institute, soon after building the first village hall in 1925, made a tennis court next door to the new building – later this area was to form part of the hall's car park. This may have been another Tennis Club, for the rules of this club (date unknown) were that 'The president of the W.I. to be an ex-officio member of the Committee together with eight others, three of whom must be members of the W.I.' The annual subscription was to be ten shillings (50p.) a year or a monthly fee of five shillings (25p.); there were reductions for families, provided they were all living in the same house. There is no longer a tennis club in the village, though there are many people with tennis courts where games are played regularly. There is now a very active indoor tennis club that meets three times a week in the village hall.

BOSHAM OLD ENGLISH BOWLING CLUB

After more than eighty years, the Bowling Club in Bosham is still playing on the grounds behind the Berkeley Arms given to them by Mr. Albert Eadie, the Lord of the Manor, some time before 1923, the latter being the date that was inscribed at the base of the original pavilion. Mr. Eadie also donated a silver cup which was known as 'The Bosham & Selsey Challenge Cup' but is a now Singles Trophy for Bosham Members.

Formed in 1911, the Club originally had its headquarters in the Berkley Arms, while the original bowling greens were behind the old bakehouse, now the private house called Loafers in Critchfield Road. The Club is still a member of the Old English Bowling Association though there are not many members of this league left now. After the 2nd World War, during which the Club went into abeyance, fixtures had to be played on opponents greens until 1959, when the bowling greens were re-turfed and in 1962 a new pavilion was built. To enhance the social side of club life, this pavilion was enlarged in 1993 and included the addition of a kitchen.

Gentlemen of the Old English Bowling Club in 1923

BOSHAM, CHIDHAM & DISTRICT HORTICULTURAL SOCIETY

Although one of the most successful societies in Bosham with a membership of over two hundred, it has been difficult to find any details of its beginnings since it was started in the mid-1930s. It is affiliated to the Royal Horticultural Society, where Bosham members have been extraordinarily successful when competing in the Society's annual shows in Chelsea. In 1952, Bert Delves, the gardener of Mr. P.J. Sainsbury, won the cup for the Best Collection of Vegetables at the Chelsea Show.

The Society holds an annual show, at one time held in a marquee either in Swan Meadow (part of which is now Old Bridge Meadow) or on the recreation ground behind the village hall. Today the annual show is held in two buildings, the village hall and the school, where not only are there cups and prizes for plants, fruit, vegetables and flower arrangements, but also for cookery, embroidery, photography and painting.

The Society meets monthly in Bosham village hall, where there are regular competitions for seasonal vegetable and plants, as well as for cookery and flower arranging. There is also a lecture given on subjects of interest to gardeners. There was a time when the monthly meeting alternated between Bosham and Chidham – in Chidham the meetings were held in the fruit room of Chidmere, by kind permission of the Baxendale family, whose gardener was a regular prize-winner of the monthly and annual competitions. With an annual subscription of only £4, it remains a very popular organisation to which to belong.

BOSHAM FLOWER CLUB

This club was started in about 1977 by Mrs. Iris Turnbull, who recognised the need for such a group in the village. Over sixty people arrived for the inaugural meeting in the village hall. There was already a church flower arrangers' guild within the organisation of the church but this could not answer the growing desire for something wider. With many similar clubs starting throughout the country, the Club became a member of the Sussex area branch of the National Association of Flower Arranging Societies (NAFAS) who were able to give much guidance in forming such clubs. Monthly meetings are held in the village hall when demonstrators, usually drawn from the NAFAS approved list of flower-arranging speakers, are organised. There are also monthly competitions, usually with a theme, and there is a sales table where all manner of items pertinent to flower arranging can be purchased. Workshops are also arranged when the art of flower

Bert Delves, gardener to Mr P J Salisbury with the cup for the Best Collection of Vegetables, Bosham Chidham & District Horticultural Socity August 1952

arranging is taught by a qualified NAFAS instructor.

The members of the Club have entered arrangements in the annual Chelsea Flower Show in London as well as taking part in many local events, such as the biennial Flower Festival in Chichester Cathedral. There have also been local flower festivals, when the Club has been allowed to decorate private houses, the takings from which have been given to charity.

BOSHAM YOUTH CENTRE

One of the more recent additions to village activities has been the Bosham Youth Centre. Opened on the 19th July 1993, as the result of the efforts of Peter Browning and Rosemary Griffin, such is the enthusiasm of Bosham's young people that it was not long before the building had to be enlarged to cope with the numbers. The land on which the centre was built is on the edge of the football pitch and has been leased for twenty eight years from the Bosham Parish Council. The centre is managed by a trust composed of residents in the village. Members are divided into two age groups; the nine-to-twelve year old section meet on Wednesday evenings, while on Tuesday and Thursday evenings the thirteen-to-eighteen year olds meet. The clubroom has a computer with hi-fi facilities, a bar (serving soft drinks) a library, pool and table tennis tables, while in the much used kitchen, cookery lessons are organised regularly. Penny Forman, a West Sussex County Council Youth Leader, organises the various activities for the young people. It is a thriving concern – one of the successful enterprises to be opened in the village in recent years, channelling as it does the energies of the teenagers into worthwhile projects.

203

THE MONDAY CLUB

On November 22nd 1965, in St. Nicholas Hall at Broadbridge, the first meeting was held of the Bosham Monday Club for the over 60s. It has proved a wonderful way for the senior citizens of the village to enjoy the company of others of their own age for a few hours every Monday afternoon. Initially the members paid 6d. (2$^1/_2$ p) a week for a cup of tea and a biscuit. There is, too, some form of entertainment such as a visiting speaker or bingo as well as a weekly raffle. A rota system of drivers was arranged so that those who could not get themselves to the meeting unassisted, were picked up and taken home by car. In 1971, the Bonhomie Club donated the first minibus to the Club. Driven by volunteers, this bus is of great help to members for in addition to the Monday afternoon journeys the bus does twice-weekly shopping trips into Chichester and to local doctors' surgeries. But there arose the problem of finance to maintain this new vehicle, for even with contributions made by various organisations, and the donations made by members when they use the minibus, the amount raised was insufficient to maintain it.

Some years ago, members and helpers formed a group calling themselves the Old Timers initially to entertain members. This group proved highly popular and it was not long before they were entertaining other similar clubs in the district; excellent fund raisers for the minibus. Today the Old Timers are able to contribute something in the order of one thousands pounds a year towards the upkeep of the bus. The entertainment follows the style of the old Edwardian music halls and includes the songs from those far-off days. When a minibus comes to the end of its life, there has always been an organisation available to provide a replacement – the club is now on its fourth vehicle.

Parties are organised for members to see plays and go to other entertainments in the area as well as group holidays, although it is necessary to hire a coach if the numbers exceed the capacity of the minibus. There is now a membership of over fifty and is the highlight of the week for the village's senior citizens, who might otherwise have a lonely time.

An engraving from an early parish magazine

THE PENNY ROYAL
Bosham's Open-Air Theatre

For seven years from 1983, Bosham had its own very successful outdoor theatre. Maggie Pollock takes up the story of how it all began.

'The sundial stands on the thrust stage of the Penny Royal Theatre in our garden with these words on its face "Horas Non Numero Nisi Serenas" [I only count the hours which are sunny] which are of some import when it comes to open-air theatre! The stage itself is on land which, before we built the theatre, grew asparagus and raspberries. In the summer of 1982 I suggested grassing over this whole area for easier maintenance so as to allow more time for sailing. 'It would make a lovely little theatre' said my husband, John, 'just the right shape with hedges bordering and facing the setting sun'. This crazy idea was soon sounding exciting and a one

hundred and seventy five seat professional open-air theatre began to take shape. We would have a month long season playing nightly in August with a matinée on Thursdays.

'Our architect and builders worked in the spring of 1983 and were ready just in time for two charity performances that year: Aubrey Woods giving his performance from Mapp and Lucia by E.F. Benson and the Chichester Players production of Joseph Andrews by Fielding, proceeds of both going to the Chichester Festival Theatre.

'Our first full four week professional repertory season came in August, 1984, with director, stage manager, designer, set makers, costumiers, stage hands and actors. All were paid at the Equity rate, while accommodation was found for them in the village. We were looking for

The Penny Royal Theatre in the garden of Trippet Meadow

205

modern plays with small casts in our endeavour to break even financially with expenses and anticipated income. Our first production was a double bill – the first play A Village Wooing by G.B. Shaw, had a palm-court trio playing, followed by The Twelve Pound Look by J.M. Barrie. The second half of the season was a new play, Bodies by James Saunders. The actors were surprised, but soon happy, to find that the theatre was in our back garden and that, combined with glorious weather, encouraged us to consider a second year.

'We presented six seasons in Bosham with a total of seventeen plays and one musical. It was good fun and quite a challenge to select two plays each year that we could cross-cast using the same actors. When we felt we had out grown our small garden with limited parking and other facilities, we arranged for two seasons at the open air Weald and Downland Museum at Singleton.

'Why did we call the theatre 'Penny Royal'? The herb pennyroyal is reputed to banish melancholy and discourage midges. Could one ask for anything more on a summer evening?'

The Penny Royal Theatre has also presented three historical plays in Bosham church, all relating to the history of the village and the Bayeux Tapestry - The King who got his Feet Wet by Charles Gattey and King Harold and King William by John Pollock.

In addition Penny Royal Publications published two books, written by John Pollock, entitled Bosham: Ecclesia and Harold Rex.

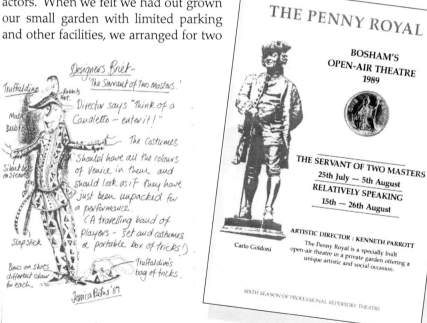

OLD BRIDGE MEADOW

The main road from Chichester to Portsmouth, known as the Turnpike Road, later the A27, was part of the main south coast road from Dover to Plymouth. In the 1970s the section of the A27 between the White Swan (at the Bosham crossroads) and Chidham was straightened, to be followed later by the building of a completely new A27 bypass and the re-numbering of the old A27 as the A259. As a result of all this road building, a short cul-de-sac was left and named Old Bridge Road. In addition, one and a half acres of unusable land was left between the old and new roads. Because this small meadow had previously been farmland, where crops had grown and animals grazed, the soil was particularly fertile. In 1999, some enterprising local residents, encouraged by the Parish Council, formed a group calling themselves the Friends of Old Bridge Meadow and set about turning this area into a wild flower meadow and recreational area with the Broadbridge stream running through the centre. Hundreds of years earlier, this stream had been diverted from the main waterway, just south of Racton Mill and a few yards north of the meadow, in order to feed Broadbridge and the Quay Mills. Recently the Friends have made the stream more attractive to flora and fauna by clearing the area of débris and reshaping the banks. With the support of the Parish Council and of the Lions Club of Southbourne, many social events have been organised by the Friends, particularly during the summer months, with concerts and community activities. At Christmas each year a party is held under the direction of members of the Salvation Army when carols are sung around a well decorated tree, the latter giving much pleasure to passers-by over the festive season. Seating has been donated by the Parish Council and the Lions Club, while trees and native species of flowers are being planted to make the area a very pleasant corner of the village. As a result of all these activities, the Friends have raised considerable sums of money both for the further development of the meadow and for local charities.

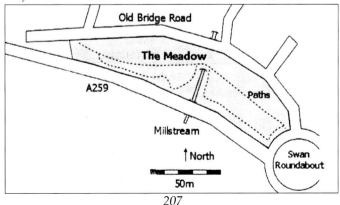

SCIENCE of THOUGHT

Tucked away in the trees between the old turnpike road and the recently built A27 dual carriageway, both of which run between Chichester and Portsmouth, is Bosham House. This is the former home of Henry Thomas Hamblin, dubbed the 'Saint of Sussex' A successful optician in London's West End, Hamblin felt a need for a more spiritual life, his message being that 'if we change our thoughts, thinking only positive, good thoughts, we change our lives'. He took a fourteen-year lease on Kenwood a house on the main road in Bosham, now run as a bed and breakfast lodge, and commenced his writings. In 1921 he published his first magazine 'The Science of Thought Review, which has been a regular feature of the Hamblin Trust ever since. This magazine has now been renamed 'New Vision', and has a circulation by donation or membership, of over one thousand. Hamblin also wrote a number of books which continue to be sold all over the world, as well as a spiritual course available to students, of whom over eight hundred took part. This course has now been published as a book called 'The Way of the Practical Mystic – the Hamblin Spiritual Course'.

In 1926, Hamblin bought the meadow next door to Kenwood and built Bosham House, where he remained until his death in 1958, but the work that he commenced seventy three years ago still continues. In 2004, Hamblin Hall was built in the grounds of the original house as a new meeting and treatment centre which has increased the facilities available both spiritually and physically, amongst the latter being yoga and tai chi. Liz Medler, who runs the centre, 'has no hesitation in labelling Hamblin "a saint" because of his humility.....but he also had a burning light within him'. The work of Henry Hamblin is continually expanding with regular organised discussions, while within the walls of the new centre more and more people are coming for spiritual refreshment in this materialist world. Hamblin's grandson, John Delafield, is still much involved in the organisation.

CHAPTER 15

Conjectures, Legends and Ghost Stories

DID ST. PAUL COME TO BOSHAM?

In about 1975, Mrs. Eva Purser was being driven along Delling Lane in Bosham. When the car reached the corner of Green Lane, Mrs. Purser volunteered the information that, in her childhood, (she was born in 1886) Green Lane was called St. Paul's Walk because, so she was told, it was where St. Paul landed when he came to England. Mrs. Purser was a grand-daughter of a former baker in Bosham and although not born in Bosham, had been brought to the village as a baby and had lived here until her marriage. She was a fund of information of events and characters in the area; a real Bosham-phile.

In the Marlipins Museum at Shoreham is a copy of a map, hand painted on wood circa 1724, the original of which is now in the East Sussex Records Office. This maps shows the centre of the village as an island with, what would appear to be, a canal running from the top of the old school Creek, along Stumps Lane, Walton Lane, Crede Lane, Green Lane and then into Delling Lane. The fields and houses alongside these five roads are all approximately 6 feet [1.8 metres] higher than the roads along which they lie. The

northern point of the 'canal' is Broadbridge Mill. The western flow of the canal appears to follow the route of the existing brook as it is today.

As there is no natural water course to that part of the village which the Romans are known to have occupied, it is almost certain that it was they who built the brook. This waterway leaves the natural water course at Ratham Mill, passes through the old Broadbridge Mill and flows down through the village to the west of Delling Lane through Broadbridge Farm, alongside Brook Avenue and then in front of the Millstream Hotel. From there it flows behind the United Reformed Church and to the west of all the houses that are situated to the west of Bosham Lane, along the western boundary and about 6 feet [1.8 metres] higher than the grounds of the Manor House gardens. From there it runs into the creek through the waterwheels of the mill on the Quay, now the Bosham Sailing Club. Level with the brook on the western side of the Manor House grounds, there is the old mill pond, now largely overgrown, fed by the brook.

With the long sun hours and

ROMAN CANAL

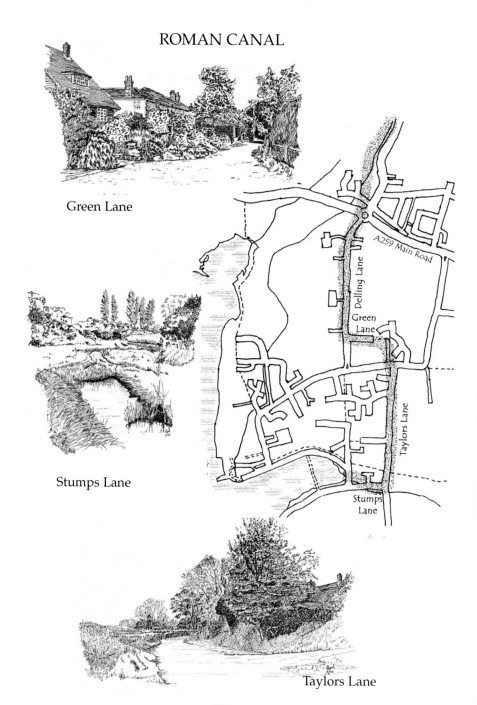

Green Lane

Stumps Lane

Delling Lane

A259 Main Road

Green Lane

Taylors Lane

Stumps Lane

Taylors Lane

excellent clay soil, the corn grown along the coastal plain east of Portsmouth was of the finest both in quality and quantity and in fact fed some of the Roman armies of north-west Europe. While certainly some of this corn would have been grown in Bosham, the majority of it would have been grown in the surrounding area. It would then have had to be carted down to the quay at Bosham for shipment across the Channel. What better way of doing this than to have pulled empty vessels up to the Broadbridge Mill area, loaded them there and then let them drift down with the flow of the water along the western canal/brook and into Chichester Harbour.

In 1962, the remains of a Roman trading vessel was discovered in the Thames when an underpass was being built at Blackfriars Bridge. She was 60 feet [18.4 m.] long and 20 feet [6.15 m.] wide and built on the Thames of timber which originated possibly from the Greenwich area. A replica of her has been built. A vessel of this size could have navigated a Bosham canal if it was the same width as the present roads.

When the suggestion was put to Maurice Hall, the author of 'Bosham and Its Berkeley Barons', that there could have been a Roman canal running in

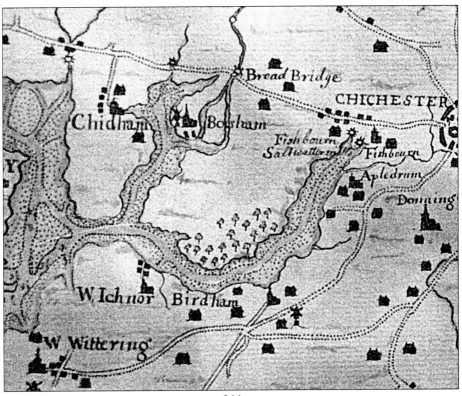

211

front of his 17th century house, Tremylet's, at the end of Green Lane, he said that not only had he found what he considered the remains of a quay alongside a stream at the bottom of his garden, but, in 1978, he had found the remains of a Roman anchor in the area. Hall subsequently piped the stream to prevent water overflowing into his garden, which it had been doing.

North-east of Maurice Hall's find, in the area of Broadbridge Farm, in the mid-19th century a Roman villa and amphitheatre were found underneath the farm's chicken houses. There was a story that this was probably the villa of a local governor of the area. It would have been about equidistant between the two sections of the canal. In the 2nd Epistle of St. Paul to Timothy, Chapter 4, verse 21, St. Paul refers to greetings to St. Paul from 'Pudens and Linus and Claudia'. It has been suggested that Claudia was the daughter of Tiberius Claudius Togibudnus (43–73 AD) and named after the Roman emperor, Claudius, who reigned from 41-54 AD and who landed in England in 43 AD, the year of the Roman invasion of Britain.

Further south, on Walton Lane, at the top of Taylors' Lane, in the deeds of one of the Creed Cottages, a jetty is marked.

Mr. R.A. Airton, in the November 1975 edition of Bosham Life wrote

'While I am unable to throw any light on the references to St Paul's Wharf, it is my opinion following examination of the excavations which took place during the recent building of the two houses in Green Lane [High Bank and Arana] that Green Lane and Delling Lane were tidal and navigable channels during the first millennium......'. In the following month, Mrs. Helen Reid of Farm Cottage, Greenacre, School Lane, (a road at right angles to the eastern end of Green Lane), wrote that St. Paul's Wharf was not in Green Lane but at the end of where the ground rises behind Greenacre in School Lane. Further she added that the Roman wall in the garden of Parker's Pound (a 17th century house in Walton Lane where Roman artefacts have been found) is due east of the site of the Wharf.

While there is little evidence that St Paul (3 – 67 AD) ever came to Britain, it is perfectly conceivable that the Romans did build a canal from Stumps Lane to Broadbridge Mill connected to the brook, which would have resulted in the centre of Bosham becoming an island. It is also possible that this canal was in continuous use until the 17th century or that at some time prior to the mid-17th century this canal was restored and would account for the waterway being shown on a number of maps of this time.

A VISION as SEEN & TOLD by PENELOPE RYCROFT

Towards the end of the Rev. Bransby-Jones' term as Vicar of Bosham (1961) Richard and Pen Rycroft had Pen's cousin, George Hooker from Ireland, to stay with them at their house 'Cossick' on Shore Road. All three went to the 9.30 service in Bosham church. It was a dull autumn day and the Rev. Gordon Bearman, (Curate 1951 - 1968) preached the sermon.

At the end of the morning service, as George, Richard and Pen came out of the church, George took Pen's arm and asked if anything unusual had happened to her whilst there. Upon Pen giving an answer in the affirmative, Richard suggested that Pen and George went straight back to Cossick and in different rooms drew and wrote what they had both experienced. This they did and found that their stories tallied exactly in relation to the Saxon period but that George had not had the Victorian experience. They were so intrigued by this that they phoned the vicar, Bransby, knowing his keen historical interests, and took their stories and drawings around to him later that day. This is the story as told by Pen:

'During the sermon my attention wandered and I began to wonder what the hole on the right side of the chancel arch could have been, for it was too large to have been a fault in the stonework. Suddenly the church of today faded and from behind the rush screen on the top of Dicul's crypt [now known as The Crypt], I saw a hand come out and give something to a monk standing close to the arch and who was dressed in a brown habit with a white rope belt. He blessed what he had received and put it into the hole in the stonework. The floor of the church was flush with the round stone bases at the foot of the chancel arch, only about three or four feet below the top of Dicul's cell and consisted of beaten earth covered thickly with rushes. The rise to the short chancel was gradual and covered with animal skins. The chancel was shorter than it is today with a windowless east wall. On each side of the chancel was a plain wooden bench with monks either sitting on them or standing in front of them. The altar at the back of the chancel was made of rough hewn wood and had a plain wooden cross with no particular carving on it. In front of it were strewn skins. Neither of us can remember seeing any candles.

'To the left of the chancel arch was a 'pulpit' of rough cut wood with posts at each corner joined by a white rope very similar to those worn by the monks in their habits. On this were about three logs on top of each other as well as some sort of platform. There was a monk standing in the pulpit. There were several people in the nave, mainly men dressed in dull coloured clothing.

'There was a bench alongside the wall of Dicul's crypt and four or five people were sitting on this with the tops of their heads or hoods very nearly level with the ceiling of the crypt. As I watched, a little man came in from my left, that is through the north door which appeared to be nearer to us than it is today and he was driving two Maltese type goats in front of him with another animal following. I had no recollection of any aisles as there are today. The little man genuflected as he passed the altar and then went out of the door on the right. I got the impression that it was evensong that I was attending. I also got the feeling that there were people congregating outside the church waiting to have a slightly clandestine funeral and that they were longing to get somebody safely buried inside or something similar. I could not get any impression of what it was, except that these people were in mediaeval dress, particularly one or two gentlemen dressed largely in black. One had a sort of broad-brimmed conical hat, a cloak and longish hair and he kept popping in and out obviously very agitated. I said to Richard a couple of times that I had a feeling that there were people congregating outside who were longing for us to finish our modern day service, so that they could come in and take possession of the church.

'The roof of the church had wooden rafters and some sort of rush thatching and not much else but as we tended to be looking

down and watching the little man going across with his sheep, looking at the people in the body of the church and the monks, neither of us would like to swear to this. I think there were four to five monks on each bench. And then there was the chap who was standing down beside the hole in the pillar and receiving these little wax figures. George saw him receive two and I saw him receive, I think, it was three or four. These arms came out from behind these really rough sort of rush screens that seemed to be standing up there and we both of us had a strong feeling that there were lepers or sick people permitted there who were not allowed to mix with the other people on the floor of the church. But these sick people appeared to have these little wax effigies with marks on them, presumably indicating where their sores were. I can see one now, a very sort of skinny emaciated bare arm come round the screen and the monk took whatever it was and he blessed it with the flat of his hand and then put it into the hole in the arch. The wax figures were two to three inches inch high and very slim so as to enter the hole easily. The congregation, if that is what they were, of about twelve to fifteen people, just stood or walked around for there were no seats. I cannot tell you what happened beyond what I have said already nor could I tell where it was. We have been questioned

214

by Bransby and various people on this but neither of us could say. I could almost pinpoint the date as early 11th century because that was when the church was that size.

'It is a job to say the sort of impression we got from what we saw. I think that it has created very much interest but naturally neither of us have talked to a lot of people – you know it isn't the sort of thing we talk about readily but a lot of people have remarked on the fact that both of us saw it in colour. It is said that quite often when this sort of thing occurs you tend to see it rather like a photograph in black and white and not in colour which surprises us because obviously there was colour and I can't understand why it should be so unusual to note colour.

'Then I came back through to the Victorian period with a heavy rood screen across the Saxon arch and I got the impression of deep red velvet or plush curtains all dusty and dark hanging there, while pews and seats had appeared in the church.'

Shortly after this incident, Bransby and a medical friend, [the surgeon Mr. Hermon Taylor] put a gastroscope [an instrument with a little tiny light on the end which, when swallowed, a surgeon can look around one's stomach or lungs] down the hole in the Saxon arch and found traces of wax in the bottom. From this they supposed that the monk had been receiving wax effigies from the sick – possibly lepers – from behind the rush screen and the monk had placed them in the hole in the belief that the sick would be cured by this action.

The chapel of All Hallowes above the crypt was not turned into a chapel until 1959 – before that there was just a plain flat cement floor.

The LEGEND of the BOSHAM BELL

Many years ago there were frequent raids on coastal villages, particularly at Bosham, by Vikings, Danes, Norsemen or just plain pirates. When the villagers got warning of such a raid, they all, with their animals and valuables, sought refuge in the church, barring the windows and doors. Almost certainly there would have been some sort of watch kept from a tower standing in the area of where the church tower is today.

Usually the raiders went through the village stealing anything they wished and then went on their way. But on this one occasion, so the story goes, the Danish pirates broke down the church door and stole one of the church bells. Taking the bell off down the harbour in one of their boats, the bell fell through the bottom of the boat at a place now called Bell Pool. The pirates went off without the bell.

The inhabitants of the village were told that if they wanted to recover their bell from below the waters, they must procure a team of pure white heifers with which to do so. This they did by tying the bell to the animals. Slowly the heifers hauled the bell to the surface. Then, quite suddenly, when almost clear of the water, the rope snapped and the bell fell back into the sea. It was discovered that one of the heifers had one black hair on its fetlock.

In the 1930s, a fisherman by the name of John Mant regularly took his family down to Pilsey Island, a beach off Thorney Island, for his children to swim and play in the sand. On one occasion when the tide was particularly low, he noticed that in the sand there was what appeared to be the corner of a bronze bell sticking out. When he told some of his chums about this sighting, they admitted that they too had seen this piece of bronze. Was this the lost bell?

The emblem of the Bosham Sailing Club is a bell.

The GHOST OF AMELIA IDLE

by Sheila Barton of 'Loafers', Bosham Lane

Do we believe in ghosts? Or should we call them apparitions or spirits?

When I came to Bosham to live in 1970, sadly only at weekends at that time, I was told by Miss Edith Coward at the then Bosham 'Stores' of course, you know you have a friendly ghost at Loafers..... if you are interested I will tell you about her one day when I am not busy'.

Later in the day when I told my husband he said: 'Well, actually, after I bought the house in 1957 the former owner did tell me that there was a ghost! I decided that when I opened the front door on dark winter nights I would be ready with the words 'I'm the new owner, I hope we shall get along well together'. But he was never tested.

News of this supposed third party in our household did not worry us but we did become more interested when our middle son, then aged fourteen, told us he had seen an elderly lady in his bedroom one night (he did not know about the ghost rumour).

So I decided to try and find out more. I wrote to the previous owner who replied 'Yes, I certainly saw her sitting by the big fireplace in the sitting room, the description is the same as the one your son gave. Several people, staying in the cottage, heard her go upstairs and into my son's room.... but nobody ever heard her come down. My bedroom door was often opened at night. The strange thing is, although I was alone in the cottage a great deal, I wasn't nervous of her, she must have been a friendly ghost because I never experienced that cold atmosphere associated with the occult........ later a friend of my son was staying with us and about 10 o'clock one night he came running downstairs

216

looking slightly shaken and said someone or something had put a hand on his shoulder. We had not told him about the ghost'.

Edith Coward was a fount of information and told me that our mysterious visitor was Madame Idle, formerly Amelia Collins of Bosham, who died in 1879, aged 81, having been the mistress of the 4th Marquess of Hertford for many years. She was left a fortune by her lover, and returned to Bosham from Paris in the 1860s and distributed largesse to members of her large family and their children, several of whom lived in the village. Our home was lived in by one of them and perhaps that is why she visits us!

Edith Coward lived in Berkeley Cottage and she said she sensed the ghost from the day she moved in in 1957

and she and her sister always called her Granny Collins. She had in fact never seen her, only heard her.

Eva Purser, the grand-daughter of one of the village bakers who operated from 'Loafers' remembers seeing a little old lady in grey in the small upstairs room at Loafers and that 'she always ran past the door quickly as she was frightened of her'.

Hugh Selwyn Lloyd who lived in the Manor House at the turn of the century before moving to The Grange in 1914 (now the Millstream Hotel) wrote in his diaries that he saw the ghost of a woman in grey whilst he was returning from Dell Quay by boat one evening after having tea with the vicar of Itchenor.

Selwyn Lloyd also recalled seeing the ghost of Edward Bennett who lived

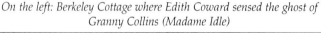

On the left: Berkeley Cottage where Edith Coward sensed the ghost of Granny Collins (Madame Idle)

in Manor Farm, renamed the Manor House in 1888, sitting in the window of a Manor House bedroom where he had died waiting for the return of his only son from sea. The Bennetts were related to Amelia Idle.

When Amelia Idle returned to Bosham from France she rented Church Farm House, opposite the Millstream Hotel, and must have seen her family frequently. However, she later moved to Shopwyke Hall and both the former owner, Philip Harris, and present owners Patrick and Maggie Burgess, have stories of people seeing her ghost there. Philip Harris says that a cleaning lady saw an apparition in the drawing room standing 'in' the grand piano who then walked past her and up the stairs.

The new owners have not seen her but a year or two ago they had a young teenage girl (who did not know the story) visiting them who exactly described the lady standing 'in' the piano. In both descriptions she was said to be wearing Paris fashions with red heels to her shoes! [Madame Idle was known to have worn red shoes frequently.]

And where does this leave us? As always with any talk of the paranormal one is full of speculation. To us Amelia Idle is a friendly visitor whom we have yet to meet but we would be most interested to hear from anyone in Bosham who may have similar stories to tell.

The GHOST of LADY (WINIFRED) ALLEN

Lady Allen, wife of Sir Hugh Allen, purchased the area now known as Bosham Hoe in 1919. In 1937 she built, at the entrance to the estate, a Norfolk thatched house, which she named 'The Hoe'. Here she lived until her death in 1966. The executors of her estate sold the house in 1967 to Mr. and Mrs. Anthony Williams who had lived in the house, 'Wolves Copse', opposite 'The Hoe' and had known Lady Allen.

The Williams proceeded to renovate the house, which included the removal of the thatch, of which Lady Allen had been very proud, and it's replacement with terracotta roof tiles.

One day the workmen in the house were confronted by an elderly lady who told them that they had done enough damage to her house and were to get out immediately. This they did. The Williams on returning to the house found the work force in the garden, refusing to return to their jobs. Their description of the elderly lady exactly fitted that of Lady Allen. Subsequently Anthony Williams 'met' Lady Allen frequently on the stairs. Anthony Williams died in October, 2000, his wife having predeceased him. The new owners, although they have undertaken many alterations and renovations to 'The Hoe' have not, so far, met Lady Allen.

A CONJECTURE
- A Saxon quay at the northern end of Tuffs Hard, Bosham Hoe.

At the southern end of Lighters Field on Bosham Hoe, there are the remains of a wall made from stone that is not native to the area. This wall, where it is visible, stretches in a semi-circular line from a point 28 feet [8.6 m.] from the northern end of the concrete of Tuffs Hard for 132 feet [40.6 m.] The whole wall is not visible but there is enough to show the line of the stones. Again a dowsing expert elicited the information that, in her opinion, this wall was a 9th century Saxon quay, in use in the 9th, 10th, 12th, 14th and from 15th to the 19th centuries. There is certain to have been trading into and out of the harbour after the Romans left in the 5th century; also we know the Danes and the Vikings attacked Chichester in 894-5, so there is every possibility that the Saxons could have had a quay at that point. Furthermore, it is known that there were many occasions over the centuries when there was insufficient water at Dell Quay for vessels to reach the upper areas of the harbour and it was necessary to unload goods and transfer them into lighters at Lighters Field (hence the name) in order

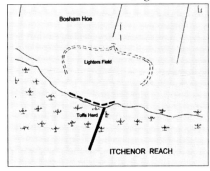

to get them to Dell Quay. Or, as has been recorded elsewhere, goods were unloaded at Lighters Field and taken overland by horse and cart to Chichester. There are large areas of gravel hard standing around Tuffs Hard.

An order was made during the reign of James 11 (reigned 1685-88) that all goods coming into Chichester Harbour must go through customs at the port of Dell Quay - so this order, combined with the times of low water levels, could account for the use of this 'quay' in the 17th, 18th and 19th centuries as a transfer point. There is even evidence that there may have been a small customs post on Lighters Field.

A sketch of what the quay might have looked like in centuries past

A CONJECTURE
Some boat shaped indentations

On the south shore of Furzefield Creek, north of the oak woods on Bosham Hoe, amongst the saltings are a number of indentations of various shapes and sizes. There is one thing that they all have in common - they are all boat shaped.

An experienced archaeological dowser has recently practised her art on some of these indentations. Two of the biggest shapes, one 24 feet 6 inches x 10 feet 6inches, [7.5 x 3.2 m.] the other 32 feet x 15 feet 6 inches [9.8 x 4.7 m.] with the indentations respectively 16 inches and 8 inches deep [0.4 x 0.2 m.], appear to be the remains of 4th century Roman vessels. How, one has to ask, have these recesses remained for two thousand years with no vegetation growing anywhere within the indentations. The Romans painted the hulls of their boats with bitumen; bitumen does not deteriorate nor will any plant grow above such material. According to the Oxford English Dictionary, the definition given for bitumen is 'naturally-occurring asphalt from the Middle East'; indeed the oil wells from which the Romans obtained this substance for their ships were recently found in the area of Ur of the Chaldees in Iraq.

Two of the other boat-shaped indentations, respectively 6 feet 6 inches and 7 feet 3 inches long [2.0 x 2.2 m.], in the area have produced evidence that they are 15th century with one 14th century boat 42 feet [12.9 m] long. All wooden vessels, until quite recently, had their hulls painted with tar and nothing but a substance containing an element of silver would ever adhere to such vessels.

The Romans would have found Furzefield Creek an excellent anchorage protected as it is from the prevailing south westerly winds. There is also evidence that the Romans did make use of this area with the finding of Roman mortar in the area. It is also conveniently situated between Fishbourne and Bosham, both areas of

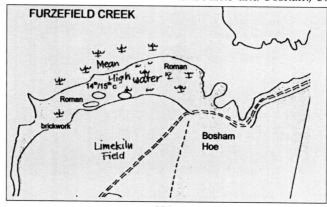

FURZEFIELD CREEK

Mean
High water
14"/15"c
Roman
brickwork
Roman
Limekiln Field
Bosham Hoe

Roman occupation. The brick works only a few yards around the corner from the 24 feet 6 inches [7.9 m.] vessel, may also have originated in Roman times and the tiles and bricks made there would have been shipped by water from the kilns. There are other Roman brick works in Chichester Harbour and all are situated along the shore for easy movement to wherever the bricks and tiles were required. There are also similar boat shaped indentations in other parts of the harbour.

Boat shaped indentations remaining unchanged over the years

CHAPTER 16

Songs & Poems of Bosham

GHOSTS OF BOSHAM

Dear ghosts of sailor men who haunt our creek,
When you return who is it that you seek?

With puzzled stare a Saxon peasant stands
And gazes speechless at the changing lands
That once he tilled so patiently and he
Fished for his food a living from the sea
Nor ever asked for, or could wish for more.

A Viking warrior rushing in to raid
Hell bent on looting, pauses, half afraid,
No timid serfs to conquer and subdue?
Seaward he turns and vanishes from view
Leaving a wake of churning foam behind.

Pale the moon, and dim her waning light,
A bearded smuggler landing late at night
His brandy casks, swings his lantern high
And gasps with fright, because he cannot spy
The well worn pathway to his hiding place.

Swiftly a crafty monk in robes of brown
His portly figure girdled, hurries down
To show a cautious light. But filled with fear
The smuggler flees and is no longer there.
Cursing, the wily monk returns to prayer.

A sailing ship calls in to land the grain
Against the quayside but it is in vain.
Gone are the bollards that the sailors knew
Could berth a ship, manned by a weary crew
Who storm tossed sought the shelter of a port.

The Men of Bosham fishers of the deep
A watch upon their oyster beds must keep
Then windblown, ruddy, tanned by summer sun
They sit and drink after their work is done
And talk in Sussex voices warm and brown.

A young blonde boy comes sailing his boat,
Blue spotted kerchief knotted round his throat.
He hears the water sing its joyous song
Careless and carefree as he drifts along.
Nor ever thought when war came he would not return.

Now gently, slowly on the falling tide,
Hand on the tiller, pipe in mouth must glide
*One who loved Bosham dearly.
Then he hears the bell
Ring from the little church he loved so well
Calling and calling, tolling loud and clear.

Summoned the ghosts crowd quickly down to see
Who needs a hand when landing at the quay.
And all of them are gathered there once more
To help him pull his boat home safe to shore
And welcome him into their company.

Jean Ogilvie 1974
*Patrick Ogilvie

BOSHAM BY THE SEA

There are marvels in the ocean,
There are wonders on the land,
There are sights that tear one's heart strings
Which few can understand.
Yet midst the greatest wonders,
There's a voice will always call
To the little place in England
That is better than them all.
Where!...*(Chorus) Sailing about the harbour*
Everyone will agree
That the prettiest place in all the world
Is Bosham by the sea.
The mountain peaks of Asia,
The rocky coast of Spain,
The pyramids of Egypt,
And the tow'rs that sigh with pain.
These may be very wonderful,
But back you'll always come
To the shores of dear old England
To your native place at home
Where!...   *(Chorus)*
Ours may be joy or sorrow,
Ours may be peace or pain
Yet we always hail the morrow,
That will bear us home again.
There be songs that take our mem'ries back
To scenes long past recall
But the "Home sweet home" of England
Is the sweetest of them all!
For - *Sailing about the harbour*
Everyone will agree
That the prettiest place in all the world
is BOSHAM BY THE SEA.
Sung to the tune of the Eton Boating Song.   H. Selwyn Lloyd

*Nothing ever changes - and the
Bosham Car Wash
still does very good business!*

This road
floods
each tide

Photo J. Colgate

Index